RAINCOAST CHRONICLES

Seventeen

Stories & History of the British Columbia Coast

Edited by

Howard White

HARBOUR PUBLISHING

OCT 24 1997

DOUGLAS COLLEGE LIBRARY

Copyright © 1996 by Harbour Publishing

All rights reserved. No part of this book may be reproduced in any manner without the written consent of the publisher, except in the case of brief excerpts in critical reviews and articles.

Published by
HARBOUR PUBLISHING
P.O. Box 219
Madeira Park, BC
V0N 2H0

Cover design by David Lee.
Cover painting by Gaye Hammond.
Printed and bound in Canada.

Canadian Cataloguing in Publication Data

Main entry under title:

Raincoast chronicles 17

ISBN 1-55017-142-9

1. Frontier and pioneer life – British Columbia. 2. British Columbia – History. 3. Pacific Coast (B.C.) – Social life and customs. I. White, Howard, 1945– II. Title: Raincoast chronicles seventeen.
FC3803.R344 1996   971.1   C96-910054-X
FC1087.5.R35 1996

Contents

Introduction

BY HOWARD WHITE

When *Raincoast Chronicles* started courtesy of a federal youth grant in 1972, we raised eyebrows by treating the 1950s as history, long before they had acquired a sufficiently sepia-toned air of antiquity in many peoples minds. In this issue we rush another period into history – that capricious paisley-trimmed decade of our own beginnings. On page 10 Mark Bostwick recalls an unforgettable summer spent rediscovering Vancouver Island's West Coast Trail in 1972, courtesy of a federal government grant from the notorious Opportunities For Youth program. His humorous and nostalgic account looks with fresh wonder at a period when leaders could respond to the challenge of displaced youth, not by increasing jail space, but by paying the kids to go out and create their own jobs. Plenty of that seed money fell on fallow ground – but as booming recreational use of the West Coast Trail and a greying *Raincoast Chronicles* attest – some of it took hold.

As architect of the Parliament Buildings, the Vancouver Courthouse-cum-Art Gallery, the Empress Hotel and other turn-of-the-century BC landmarks, Francis Rattenbury has a claim to being BC's favourite architect. On page 5, Robin Ward – one of BC's favourite writers on architecture – critiques one of Rattenbury's less-known works, his own family home in Oak Bay, and in so doing provides a delightfully irreverent commentary on Rattenbury's brilliant and scandalous career.

In trying to record pioneer experiences, something which has bedeviled us from the first is the invisibility of women. We know they were there standing shoulder-to-shoulder with their men, but when it came time to record the scene for posterity, often as not they were left out of the picture. One glorious exception is Hannah Maynard, who solved the problem of being left out of the picture by taking her own. The tag "Maynard photograph" is stamped all over BC's historical face, but what of the woman behind the lens? On page 20 curator Petra Watson gives a rare glimpse of this self-taught pioneer photographer, whose busy Victoria studio recorded every facet of BC life for four crucial decades from 1862 to 1912.

Among the primary factors which shaped BC are the smallpox epidemics which reduced aboriginal populations to insignificance – normally viewed as an unavoidable natural occurrence. Were the plagues really a pioneering form of biological warfare manipulated by colonial administrators to guarantee BC would come out of the colonial period white? On page 29 epidemiologist Douglas Hamilton takes a closer look at this growing controversy.

No First Nation was more severely affected by smallpox than the Sechelt Nation, whose aboriginal metropolis at Kalpalin (Pender Harbour) made them one of the great powers of the northwest coast. On page 57 Howard White, a long-time resident of Pender Harbour, ponders the ruins of Kalpalin and fills in some gaps in the history of this little-studied group.

Some issues of *Raincoast Chronicles* have been planned around themes – logging, fishing, early Vancouver, forgotten villages – while for others unplanned themes have emerged after the fact in the form of nicknames – the soft logging issue (No. 6), the E.J. Hughes issue (No. 10), etc. Maybe this one will become known as the bad medicine issue. Two of the articles deal with aboriginal health issues, while a third, *The Doctor Book* by Margaret McKirdy (page 74), revisits the day when "felons" – painful infections under the fingernail – had to be treated at home with the advice of *The Doctor Book*: "Call the patient's attention to something at the other side of the room and while he is looking away press down hard with the knife ... he will jerk and thus make the cut long enough ..." McKirdy goes on to explore not just the vastly changed world of family health care since pioneer times, but also the changed role of family values in this beautifully-written piece.

Raincoast Chronicles 17 is rounded out with Lynn Ove Mortensen's biography of August Schnarr, the legendary Knight Inlet trapper (page 41), Paul Lawson's poem "The Rock Bandits," a "recipe" for donkey boiler coffee by the late Arthur Mayse, and two short amusing stories by Jack Springs and Dick Hammond. ❖

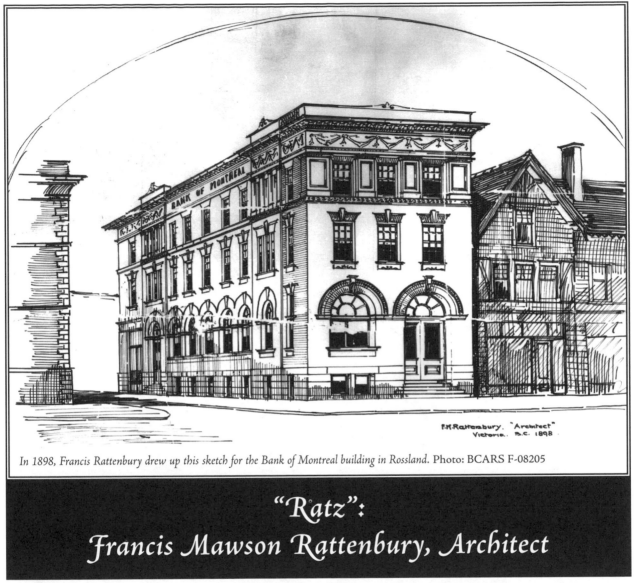

In 1898, Francis Rattenbury drew up this sketch for the Bank of Montreal building in Rossland. Photo: BCARS F-08205

"Ratz":
Francis Mawson Rattenbury, Architect

BY ROBIN WARD

Many of the Europeans who settled in Victoria in the mid- to late 1800s were opportunistic Scots, but it was an ambitious English architect, Francis Mawson Rattenbury, who gave the city its turn-of-the-century imperial character. If ever a city owed its appearance to one man, it is this one. Rattenbury's extravagant relics—especially the Parliament Buildings and the Empress Hotel, his two most photographed buildings—are prominent in an architectural heritage that includes some of the finest fin-de-siécle structures in Canada.

Rattenbury was born into a Methodist family in Leeds in 1867 and studied architecture with his two uncles, William and Richard Mawson. Lockwood & Mawson, as the uncles' firm was known before Rattenbury's apprenticeship, had made its reputation in mid-Victorian England with designs for a town hall and a model mill town built for "work, health, education, and moral instruction." But Rattenbury knew there were more exciting opportunities in Canada, where booming colonial cities brimmed with work for British-trained architects. In 1892, he sailed for Montreal.

Rattenbury gave himself a crash course in current North American styles by looking around Montreal before catching the train to Vancouver.

Within a year he had achieved astonishing early success by winning the competition for the new Provincial Parliament Buildings in Victoria. He was twenty-five years old.

When Rattenbury first sailed into Victoria's Inner Harbour in 1892 to scout out the site for the Parliament Buildings, he was inspired to create an "imperial garden of Eden." In those days visitors to Victoria arrived by sea, and Rattenbury envisioned the landlocked harbour not as a frontier town with an Indian village, but as a sort of European piazza dotted with picturesque statuary and monumental buildings—all of his own design.

To some extent he got his wish. Rattenbury was the toast of local society after his success with the Parliament Buildings and the CP Railway's Empress Hotel, one of the legendary imperial hotels. "Ratz," as he was ambiguously nicknamed, wasn't easy to work with—he played the temperamental artist when he was not given complete control of his projects and habitually fired off outrageously pompous letters to his clients if they interfered with his designs. He was given to profligate spending, noisy public tantrums and cavalier dealings with contractors and suppliers. But the Parliament Buildings and the Empress are still the centrepieces of Victoria's special architectural presence. With his design for the Crystal Garden and the CP Steamship Terminal, Rattenbury's Inner Harbour tableau was nearly complete.

In 1898, a few months after the Parliament Buildings had opened, Rattenbury married Florence Eleanor Nunn, daughter of a former British Indian Army captain. If Rattenbury thought he had gained a partner who would join in the whirl of his social life as the most prominent architect in the province, he was mistaken. Florence had enough grit to accompany him over the Chilkoot Pass during one of his wild schemes to run riverboats to the Klondike, but later she preferred to potter around in the garden of "Iechineel," the

English-born architect Francis Mawson Rattenbury gave Victoria its turn-of-the-century imperial character. Portrait circa 1924. Photo: BCARS F-02163.

This portrait of Mrs. Rattenbury (Florence Eleanor Nunn), was taken by Hannah Maynard. Photo: BCARS B-07984.

BC's first parliament buildings, known as the Bird Cages (in background), were moved to make room for Rattenbury's new parliament complex. Rattenbury appears in the centre of this 1893 photo. Photo: BCARS A-02574.

Rattenbury-designed BC Parliament Buildings under construction in the 1890s. Photo: BCARS D-05994.

Francis Mawson Rattenbury's work is well known and highly regarded in British Columbia today, but outside the province and Canadian architectural circles, the architect is a forgotten figure. In his prime, Rattenbury was an esteemed and envied member of Victoria's elite; in the 1920s his career and his domestic and social life took irreversible tumbles.

Rattenbury began building "Iechineel," his home in Oak Bay, in 1899. He was a flamboyant designer, almost always erring on the side of excess rather than understated good taste, but his home is cozy and charming, built in modest English Arts and Crafts style—the picture of domestic harmony. Florence, Rattenbury's first wife, loved Iechineel so much that when the marriage broke down she had a new home built within sight of it, and she brooded over it until she died in 1929. Glenlyon School took over the building in 1935. Photo by Robin Ward.

Oak Bay home Rattenbury began to build the following year.

What stories buildings tell. Rattenbury's Oak Bay home is picture perfect in its cozy image of rustic England, a scene of peace and contentment. And for a time, the Rattenburys were at ease here with their two children and their garden parties—"Iechineel" is an Indian word for "the place of good things." To this day, if you walk round to the back of the house, away from the carefree children's voices at Glenlyon School, which took over the house in 1935, you can sit on the shore and gaze on the islet Rattenbury bought and planted with gorse to colour the view.

But Rattenbury was never satisfied. He kept adding mock Tudor gables to the back of the house, spoiling its modest personality, much in the way that his growing self-importance began to erase whatever charm he once had. Still, with its rustic stone, leaded glass, patterned shingles and picturesque gables, Iechineel is the most attractive of all the smaller homes Rattenbury designed. While he often lacked the patience to attend to details, and was more comfortable wielding a flamboyant brush than a precise pen, he sometimes showed an instinctive ability to mellow his buildings' baronial bearing with coziness and charm.

Looking at Rattenbury's buildings and unrealized projects, one is left with the rather melancholy impression of a talent unfulfilled. His release from a plodding apprenticeship in England proved to be a creative dead end. Opportunity was there for the taking in the colonies—Rattenbury would have been lucky to land the Parliament Buildings prize in the old country, and even if he had, his uncles' firm would have taken the credit. But ultimately, he played safe with his styles. He never challenged his clients' old-world tastes any more than they encouraged him to broaden his own. Rattenbury was simply one of the legion of able British architects who prospered by building colonial works from Sydney to Singapore, and Melbourne to Montreal. In Victoria, he is remembered affectionately as a colourful fellow who designed some of the best-loved and most enduring buildings in town.

Ironically, one of those buildings was the setting for the beginning of Rattenbury's spectacular downfall. In late 1923, a dinner took place at the Empress Hotel to celebrate the commission for the Crystal Garden. Rattenbury, who was fifty-six, attended as guest of honour and was bewitched by Alma Pakenham, a wartime heroine and *arriviste*, twice married and thirty years his junior. He surreptitiously began visiting her house in James Bay where she lived as an apparently respectable piano teacher with her young son. Rattenbury made no secret of their trysts once the gossip got out. He might have retained his reputation had he been discreet, but locals drew the line when the couple began to appear together at the theatre after Florence had refused Rattenbury a divorce and, subsequently, when he tried every tactic short of murder to dispose of her. They were finally divorced in 1925. Rattenbury and Alma married but were ostracized by local society, and his career was in ruins. Percy Leonard James, the associate designer of the CP Steamship Terminal and the Crystal Gardens, sought credit for both buildings and Rattenbury had few friends left to contradict the claim.

Like many ageing empire builders, he retired to England in 1929, accompanied by Alma. But he was unknown and unfeted in his native land. In a poetic turn of events he was murdered by his chauffeur, who was also his wife's paramour, in an Agatha Christie setting in Bournemouth where he and Alma had settled. The "Villa Madeira" case caused a sensation in 1935, making the front pages of not only the Bournemouth *Echo*—"All Night Queue for the Villa Murder Trial... Sensational Allegations by the Prosecutor... Retired Architect's Death... Chauffeur accused of Murder"—but the *Times* of London. The case packed out the public viewing galleries in the Old Bailey and was the inspiration for a play, *Cause Célèbre*, by Terence Rattigan. Were it not for his well-publicized demise, Rattenbury would have ended his days in obscurity. But his work, even if only as an imperial footnote, deserves to be better known beyond the city where he made his reputation. ❖

Excerpted from Echoes of Empire: Victoria and Its Buildings, *by Robin Ward, Harbour Publishing, 1996.*

At Tsusiat Falls driftwood shelters with homey touches like hand-crafted benches, tables and a sauna suggested that other hikers were equally enthralled with the beautiful beach and freshwater pool at the base of the falls.

Opportunities for Youth, 1972, and the West Coast Trail

STORY AND PHOTOS BY MARK BOSTWICK

Across Canada during the soggy winter months of 1971 and 1972, thousands of young people living "collectively" (in shared accommodation) pushed aside the sand candles, Zig Zag papers and Grateful Dead albums, and sat cross-legged around homemade coffee tables filling in application forms for Opportunities for Youth grants. OFY had approached the chronic problem of summer unemployment with an unorthodox idea: let the unemployed themselves create jobs with government financial assistance. The concept suited the needs of a generation. Young people were in no hurry to choose careers because things were getting better, a little better, all the time. Why lock into life too soon? Better to explore, especially if the government would pay you $100 a week to do so. OFY encouraged the prevailing "do-it-yourself" ethic since any proposal would be entertained, no matter how quixotic, droll or impractical.

I immigrated to Vancouver in the summer of 1971, arriving with a rucksack, duffel bag, fifty pounds of paperback books and a small grubstake of $1,800. For a couple of weeks I scoured the bulletin boards at UBC and along West 4th Avenue looking for a place to rent or a house to share. I rejected a dank basement suite with no light and a rock band upstairs, backed out of a house full of acid freaks, and placed my hopes in getting accepted by a group of women forming a house around interests in "the NDP and Women's Studies." The seriousness of the notice implied cleaner bathrooms, more regular hours.

The core group included a student nurse, a UBC student, a fish plant worker, and an unemployed office worker. The actual occupants changed with traumatic regularity and ultimately encompassed a longshoreman/actor, a bird caller, a revolutionary on the lam, a bank teller and a blacklisted ex-teacher and mountain equipment sales representative from Colorado. The house on West 12th in Point Grey had a big kitchen, one bath (no shower), a few sticks of cast-off furniture and a relentlessly inquisitive landlady. My 90-dollar share of the rent entitled me to a small room on the main floor beside the living room. My little pad was spartan, but sufficient: a mattress on the floor, a small desk with a rented electric typewriter, bricks and boards for bookshelves, and a couple of Fillmore posters on the wall.

The lifestyle of the house was a mixture of collective fun and interpersonal tension. On Tuesday evenings the whole house hitchhiked from West 10th and Sasamat to the UBC Women's Studies lectures: Women and the Industrial Revolution, the Myth of Penis Envy, Fear of Success, Women and Canadian Literature, Alternative Lifestyles. We drank beer at the Cecil Hotel, or if it was too crowded, at the Yale or Austin. We shopped for India print bedspreads along 4th Avenue, beads on West 10th, and watched old Marx Brothers movies at the Commie Kids Flicks on Carrall Street. We took long walks in the University Endowment Lands to collect autumn leaves and initiate romances. Collectively we pasted together paper lampshades, sang folksongs, and protested the nuclear tests on Amchitka Island. We also argued over the dullness of the food (brown rice and broccoli was the house staple) and dishwashing praxis (rinsers vs dunkers). There were disputes over who cleaned the bathroom (one of the women tore out a couple of pages of *Sisterhood is Powerful* and pasted it

over the ring around the tub); whether lounging around nude was social, anti-social, or showing off; and whether forming an intimate relationship undermined the household collectivity (I had formed one with Shelly Tees, the office worker).

Homes like ours did not exist in isolation. Everyone in our house knew people living in other collectives scattered across Point Grey, Dunbar and Kitsilano, and we maintained connections through parties, romances, borrowing, bartering and sharing information. Word about Opportunities for Youth spread across this network like wildfire. My old college friend Shelagh knew Larry, who knew Mary Jane and Sudsy, who knew Ellen Rosenberg. And Ellen, a biology grad student at SFU, was reputed to be a master at preparing successful OFY applications.

Over Christmas we began devising a proposal. We had no political illusions about OFY: it was a ploy by Pierre Trudeau to buy off the revolution; it was intended to disperse angry youth into tiny projects with low pay; it was a way to appease a group of young Liberal bureaucrats with "project officer" jobs that would permit them to keep their hair long and wear blue jeans. On the other hand, my bankroll was dwindling, Shelly was tired of her office job, and OFY seemed like an attractive way to spend the summer in the country.

Our initial ideas ranged from the sublime to the ridiculous. Why not rent a boat, load it with library books and cruise the inland waters stopping in at coastal villages to promote reading? This was such a good idea we even travelled to Nanaimo to talk the Regional Library people into supporting us, but it foundered on "practicalities." None of us knew anything about boats, sailing, or libraries. The crew looked a little shaky, too. One woman was trying to decide whether to join us or take an all-nude role as a character named "Cocaine" in a local film production.

A "Trans-Canada Hiking Guide" seemed more practical: a guide to short hikes accessible from the Trans-Canada Highway. It had some tourist promotion features and would allow us to spend the summer exploring the province. Dougald MacDonald, author of *Hiking Near Vancouver*, graciously wrote a recommendation and we sent in an application.

Ellen prepared our backup application, "The West Coast Trail Project." She had spent some time at the Bamfield Marine Biology station located near the northern end of the old West Coast Life Saving Trail on Vancouver Island. The Trail, which followed the coastline south for 44 miles to Port Renfrew, was slated to be the key feature of the recently announced Pacific Rim National Park. In our application we promised to establish "information centres" at either end of the Trail, and to register hikers and provide them with information. In addition, we would mediate between the visitors and residents of Bamfield and Port Renfrew. And finally, we promised to prepare a brochure on the Trail. The woman at the local OFY office thought this one was pretty good and told us "I'll probably be calling you from Ottawa."

We waited. The hiking guide proposal got turned down. We waited some more. The house broke up, Shelly and I moved down to Larry's place at 6th and Yew where we shared two small rooms and Larry's hand coffee grinder. We talked about what we'd do if the project did not come through. Finally, in late April we received word that the West Coast Trail Project had been approved.

Ellen Rosenberg and her fiancé Michael would run the Bamfield centre. Shelly and I, along with Evelyn Williams, a stringy blonde woman from small-town BC who had attended SFU and gestalt therapy workshops on Cooper Island, would staff the Port Renfrew centre. We purchased maps of the Trail, started buying equipment at the Mountain Equipment Co-op (which was then a room above a store on 4th Avenue), and began developing a strategy for moving to the Island.

While gearing up for our departure it dawned on us that we had signed up for something more than a lark. We knew no one in Port Renfrew, had no place to stay, had never hiked the Trail, and weren't sure when OFY would send us the first installment of our grant. It was our responsibility to become instant experts on the Trail and to run the information centre seven days a week for an unknown number of hours. No one had even the sketchiest idea of how many parties hiked the Trail each week.

Nevertheless, in late May Shelly and I took the MV *Queen of Victoria* to Victoria and put our thumbs out, hoping to cover the seventy miles to Port Renfrew by nightfall. A tattooed skin diver who choked sunken deadheads for $50 a day gave us a ride to Jordan River where we sat around in the Breakers Cafe until three hippies in a pickup truck took us as far as the squatter's encampment at China Creek. A working guy in another pickup truck took us the last twenty-four miles on a dirt road to Port Renfrew.

When we got there, we were not filled with hope. The pub in the hotel above the government wharf was locked because of a power outage and the hotel had no rooms anyway since the owner was raising chinchillas upstairs. We camped on the floor of an old fishermen's dormitory next door to the pub. It had no lights; scraps of drywall hung off the walls; the floor was littered with cigarette butts, beer bottles and several stained copies of *Jesus and His Friends.*

The next morning we set out on foot to visit the BC Forest Products logging camp, hoping to get help finding accommodation. For a small community of a few hundred souls, Port Renfrew was remarkably decentralized. A few houses clustered around the elementary school, hotel, and government wharf. A little farther on we passed the BCFP residential enclave, which looked like a tiny perfect California suburb with clipped lawns and sprinklers dropped onto the wild West Coast. Down the road we passed a patch of forest with the barnlike general store almost all by itself. The road beyond the store eventually crossed the San Juan River and parallelled a beautiful long beach strewn with chalk-white driftwood. The Pacheenaht Reserve embraced the Gordon River estuary below the BCFP forest operations. After the reserve the road passed a small cluster of old houses known as "Elliott's Cabins," circumvented the dump, and continued on into the BCFP site. We did not have to walk the entire way: the local school bus driver picked us up about halfway and gave us a ride to "Elliott's Cabins." Frank Elliott, one of the town's old-timers, wasn't around but we had a long chat with Fred King, who lived next door.

King was standing in his garden smoking his pipe and listening to the radio. He was a small Scotsman with grey hair, blue eyes and a taste for philosophizing. Within minutes he was showing us his beautiful dogwood and chestnut trees, and relating long stories about his adventures as a seaman, fisherman, policeman, Hollywood ladies' man and night watchman. His living room was full of electrical gadgets including three television sets and a half dozen tea kettles. Over coffee and Peak Freans he delivered with complete certainty the prediction that within thirty years the strain on the natural environment would reach a breaking point and there would be a major crisis. He offered to loan us a copy of Velikovsky's *Worlds in Collision*.

But our needs were more immediate. We hoofed on up to the BCFP logging site: a collection of two-storey frame buildings, including several dormitories, a cafeteria, rec room and administration building. We asked to see the boss. He was not immediately available so we had a cup of coffee and a slice of homemade pie in the cafeteria while we waited.

When we were ushered into Ken Halberg's office it was obvious to us that he already knew about our mission; news travels fast in a small community and it was Halberg's responsibility to know what was going on anywhere near his domain. He had invited his forester, Stan Nichols, to sit in. We

The old Life Saving Trail had been virtually abandoned in 1954… The federal government had sent in a few teams to reconnoitre and chop away some salal, but rot and deadfall had taken their toll: cable bridges and boardwalks were often barely passable, and always dangerous.

were ingratiatingly frank and friendly, avowing that we (and the federal government) wanted to save the community from problems with hikers and hippies. We also asked if he could help us find a place to stay. To our relief, both Halberg and Nichols were receptive to the idea of an information centre. They seemed thankful we were not agents of the Sierra Club. Halberg apparently believed our motives were benign, or at least perceived us as harmless. He offered to introduce us to Art Jones, the acting Pacheenaht Band chief, who ferried hikers across the river and who might help us find a place to live.

Despite its small size, or perhaps because of it, Port Renfrew had a subtle power structure. Halberg and Art Jones represented the two strategic communities. The company was the only real local industry, they could provide plum jobs like running the boom boats or doing office work, and they had the most technical expertise and equipment. The Band, on the other hand, controlled the estuary through which many of the logs were floated into the bay to form rafts; they had lines of communication with the federal government through the Department of Indian Affairs; and they had moral status as the area's oldest inhabitants. Relations between the two leaders were marked by careful courtesy and polite respect. Halberg almost self-consciously removed his hat when we entered Art's house.

Art Jones, a large middle-aged man, was fixing a car with the assistance of a bevy of toddlers when we pulled into his yard. Over the summer we would observe that Art spent most of his time fixing something, often for us. And he usually had several youngsters in tow. After Halberg summarized our plan and our needs, he offered (once the Band elders approved) to rent us a couple of small cabins on the reserve that had been recently vacated by Band families moving into new homes. The rent was $35 a month. It was easy to say yes. In private we agreed that Art was the friendliest person we had met so far in Port Renfrew.

Shelly and I had a little clapboard cabin facing the Gordon River estuary, with two rooms and a bedroom with linoleum floors, a shower and a propane stove. Art's housewarming gift was an old radio that could pick up signals from Victoria and sometimes Vancouver. Television had not yet reached this West Coast outpost. Evelyn would live in the second cabin and share our kitchen facilities. Shelly found a satiny driftwood plank on the beach on which I inscribed "West Coast Trail

Information Centre" with a felt-tip pen. We nailed the sign over the doorway and declared ourselves "ready for business."

Two days later we had our first customers: six hippies starting out on the Trail. We had little information, but did arrange for them to get across the river in Art's aluminum boat. After a ride to Sooke on Paul Miklevic' school bus and a quick trip back to Vancouver to borrow a friend's old Econoline van, fill it with bits and pieces of furniture, and collect our two cats, we returned to Port Renfrew and established a rustic but pleasant household.

We soon learned that ritual is a large part of village life. One of our rituals was morning coffee by the river across from our cabin. Watching the world go by is a corollary ritual: observing the gulls sprint across the sky and the crabs scuttle through the old seat springs and cam shafts on the sandy bottom of the river. In the distance a man and a boy rowed upstream against the outgoing tide, seeming

Camping on the beach.

14

to chase a lazy loon across the smooth water. The breeze rustled the broomflowers behind the cabin and we could hear the roar of waves crashing along the beach down the road. Occasionally a Beaver floatplane would land on the water right in front of the cabin, bringing some important person or message to the logging camp.

We wanted for very little. Art was forever turning up with a fresh salmon, a big crab or advice on where the berries were ripening. In many ways Port Renfrew was an economy of scarcity. Not poverty: it was just that things were hard to get. The nearest towns, Sooke and Lake Cowichan, were a long distance away. If something broke, people scavenged to find something to fix it. Help was not so much a conscious act of goodwill as a kind of unconscious habit. When the battery on our borrowed van died I simply hitched a ride into Cowichan on the morning BCFP crummy and somebody in Cowichan arranged to get me back to Port Renfrew where Art's brother helped me install it.

Time in a isolated place had many measures. One kind of time was marked by the trucks heading from town to the logging camp before dawn, followed an hour later by the school bus to Sooke, then a bit later by Leonard Jones's local school bus. After a rainstorm there was just enough time to hike to the grocery store and back before the dust returned. The changing tides followed a lunar schedule: the waterline varied ten or twelve feet in a single day and tide tables were an important survival tool for hikers on the Trail. Every few days we would stand on the porch of our shack and watch the boom boats manoeuvre a raft of logs down the river and out into San Juan Bay. In many respects a calendar seemed a more appropriate timepiece than a clock.

Our next task was to hike the Trail and gather information. The old Life Saving Trail had been hacked out of the forest before the turn of the century to permit the rescue of seamen from the many ships blown against the rugged coastline by Pacific storms. The Trail was forty-four miles long, following sandstone shelves and long driftwood-littered beaches, skirting headlands and rocky spots by angling into the forest. Dozens of streams and sev-

eral watercourses large enough to be called rivers cut across the pathway. These gorges were traversed by a system of ladders, steps and the occasional rickety bridge. With the exception of the Nitinat Lake area, the only access points were Bamfield in the north and Port Renfrew on the south. Once on the Trail a party was pretty much committed to struggling through.

The old Life Saving Trail had been virtually abandoned in 1954, rendered technologically obsolete by modern communications and helicopters. The federal government had sent in a few teams to reconnoitre and chop away some salal, but rot and deadfall had taken their toll: cable bridges and boardwalks were often barely passable, and always dangerous. Some ladders were missing three or four rungs in a row. From the moment we passed the fish boundary marker on the north side of the river, we found ourselves in physical combat with nature. It took us nine hours to cover five miles of mud, deadfall, tangled roots, slippery notched log ladders and thick ferns. We fell into bed at a bivouac camp tucked into a corner of a wet, misty forest.

The second day we got our first real glimpse of the ocean as we slogged along a vast sandstone shelf, skipping across surge channels, clambering around rocks, avoiding the impassable sections by re-entering the forest. The hardest section proved to be a large blowdown with logs stretched through the forest end to end in a zigzag fashion, sometimes a couple of yards above the forest floor. One misstep and I was convinced I would disappear into the underbrush never to be seen again.

We were living off backpacker's grub, a mixture of nuts and dried fruit, salty dried soups, crackers and Kraft dinner. No matter how much we ate, our packs did not seem to get any lighter. Our shoulders were sore, our feet were constantly wet and sprouting blisters. The local insect population treated us like Sunday supper. After a little flirtation the sun got shy, retreating in the face of a thick fog and steady drizzle.

On the fourth day I heard myself chanting a phrase from Milton's *Paradise Lost* about "rocks, fens, bogs, dens" and adding "beaches, briars, boulders and slippery boardwalks." Nevertheless, we began to get our hiking legs, to make better time on the open beaches, and wisely to stop early, cook early and go to bed early.

By carefully pacing ourselves and conserving energy we were better equipped to deal with some of the obstacles. The ladders down into Logan Creek were a fright, the slippery wet slanting corduroy boardwalk between Clo-oose and Whyac was perilous. I fell off—and through—the rotting wood several times. We hired a Native boatman to get us across the foamy whirlpools at Nitinat Narrows; he was nonchalant but my knees were shaking.

Respite came at two points: Carmanah lighthouse, a small freshly painted island of civilization overlooking the grandiose verge of rugged coastline and supremely powerful ocean, and Tsusiat Falls where the cascade created a freshwater pool on a beautiful beach. Tsusiat was like one of those oases that appear out of the burning desert in a film about the Foreign Legion. The number of driftwood shelters with homey touches like hand-crafted benches, tables and a sauna suggested that other hikers were equally enthralled.

On the sixth day, having pulled ourselves across Darling Creek on a decrepit little raft, we hightailed out to the West Coast Trail Information Centre (northern branch) just outside the Bible Camp. It was empty. We had expected to meet Ellen, Michael and Evelyn coming the other way, and it

The author and his partner Shelly at the information centre they established in 1972 at Port Renfrew with an Opportunitites for Youth grant. "Visitors appeared at all hours of the day and night… More than a few prospective hikers came without shirts, shoes or food. 'I thought I could just eat berries on the way,' said one. Some welcomed our advice, some didn't."

was not until we had hitchhiked back to Port Renfrew that we learned Michael had twisted his ankle at Logan Creek and been airlifted out by a Canadian Forces helicopter.

I concluded that the Trail was no birdwalk: it required skill, resourcefulness and stamina. Clearly the pioneers who had built and manned the Life Saving Trail were a hardy bunch. Every section of the path presented new challenges, new risks, new terrain. Having spent most of my outdoor life in the high mountains, I was entranced by the deep woods, tide pools, rocky cliffs and intricate ecosystems. At the same time I was discouraged at the intrusion of "civilization" in the form of lost lumber, plastic containers, old bottles, milk cartons and shards of cloth that littered the beaches. But mainly I felt good about myself. I had experienced a genuine adventure, one which I was willing to repeat.

Back at our Centre we settled into the rhythm of life in a small, isolated community. Conscious of our delicate position in the community, we tried to remain unobtrusive while keeping all lines of communication open. Stan Nichols, the BCFP forester, invited us over to the compound for dinner several times and told us about life in the logging camps. Working one's way up the corporate ladder meant accepting a series of postings in places like Port Renfrew. He loved the outdoors, and was persuaded by our boasting to hike the Trail himself, while we came to understand from him that living through a rainy winter ("seventeen inches in three days") in Port Renfrew took a different kind of stamina. Wives, especially, suffered from the isolation.

By mid-summer the number of hikers had swelled from a trickle to a steady stream. Art was kept busy taking hikers back and forth across the Gordon River, and appreciated the fact that we steered them to him, helped them find campsites, and gave them advice about finding a phone, buying supplies and staying out of the hair of the Pacheenaht and the loggers.

For city dwellers accustomed to the staccato rhythms of urban life, the measured life of Port Renfrew was an adagio of small events. The mail came three times a week and everyone, especially Evelyn, looked forward to the long walk to the post office, partly because we were not getting along that well: a matter of personal chemistry and world view. Movie night at the school was a chance for the community to get together. The arrival of books through the Vancouver Island Library system was a regular milestone; it was much easier to get a bestseller in Port Renfrew than in Vancouver. Shelly's huckleberry pie, made from berries we picked behind the cabin, improved an entire day. The first tiny perfect strawberries from the Reserve's patch were a huge treat. Sporadic power outages provided comic relief and consternation. Having planned a grand dinner, the resourceful Mrs. Nichols was sometimes forced to turn quickly to cold cuts and homemade wine.

Our neighbours killed a black bear wounded by poachers behind our cabin. The propane stove exploded and started a fire in the insulation, nearly burning the cabin down, while a covey of hikers continued to gaze at the maps on our wall as if a house fire were a normal occurrence here in the sticks. Our two city cats became adept hunters, bringing in prizes on a regular basis. A sudden increase in gulls announced the arrival of a fish packer boat and the fishing fleet. The pub was crowded for a couple of days, then the fleet moved on. The OFY sent a woman out to check our books; she arrived in a granny dress and granny glasses, spent an hour and left satisfied. Indian

Affairs cruised into the Reserve like a visiting eighteenth-century French *intendent* and left in a cloud of dust. First the fallers, then all the loggers went on strike. The woods stopped roaring with the sound of heavy machinery, and the black bears prowled hungrily around the dump.

The big political event of the summer mounted slowly. After years of petitioning by the community, the Bailey Bridge was fixed, and a few weeks later a section of the road was paved. Suddenly Victoria seemed to be taking an interest in little old Port Renfrew. The reason became clear in mid-summer when Social Credit Premier W.A.C. Bennett called an election. Phyllis Smith, the librarian at the elementary school, arranged for Tommy Douglas, who was then the New Democratic Party MP for Esquimalt, to pay a visit. He brought Jim Gorst, the local NDP candidate, with him. When asked if the NDP's plan for socialized auto insurance wouldn't put a lot of private insurance salesmen out of work, Gorst replied, "Oh, they can go to work in government offices." Tommy Douglas intervened hastily and smoothed things over by describing his achievements in Saskatchewan and discussing local issues like school funding and Unemployment Insurance. I was convinced that Social Credit would win again, but this was not the first or last time my political predictions would be wrong. Even Jim Gorst got elected.

Meanwhile we continued to serve the hiking public from the Centre. Visitors appeared at all hours of the day and night in numbers ranging from one to twenty. We looked first at their footwear, advising those who came in running shoes, cross-country ski boots or sandals that they would find the Trail a little tough. We warned people that dogs who couldn't climb ladders were in for a surprise, that babies would be miles and days from the nearest doctor. More than a few prospective hikers came without shirts, shoes or food. "I thought I could just eat berries on the way," said one. Some welcomed our advice, some didn't. A huge troop of Boy Scouts from Arizona with a troop leader who looked like Hermann Goering dismissed our advice. They went on to appall the other hikers by hoisting the Stars and Stripes at

The fresh paint and neatly clipped lawns of the Carmanah Lighthouse was an island of civilization overlooking the grandiose verge of rugged coastline and supremely powerful ocean.

each camp, and they got seriously hung up on the surge channels at high tide.

Returning hikers often stopped in at the Centre to recount tales of daring, like the young woman who swam all the surge channels, or the fellow who dog-trotted the Trail in a couple of days. More often we listened to harrowing stories of monstrous blisters, bruised shins, hordes of mosquitoes. The little logbook held comments like: "On the boardwalk by Whyac the boards which go crossways are less slippery than those which go lengthways, but I fell twice anyways." There was universal agreement that the trip was well worth it.

Shelly and I hiked the Trail a second time, starting from Bamfield. This time we were better prepared and graced with good fortune. The weather was warm and the forest muffled the sound of our footsteps on the plank bridges. At Klanawa River, floods had broken the line to the old raft, but an athletic young woman hiking with her mother arrived in the nick of time and swam across to reconnect the cord, while her mother floated across

on an air mattress. At Darling Creek, clusters of young people were bathing and laughing in the sun. Tsusiat Falls had more conveniences. The weather just got better and better.

There was more time for discoveries. We explored the rusting remnants of the USS *Michigan* and warmed ourselves with a driftwood fire banked against a plate from the *Uzbekistan*. Outside Clooose we poked around an old cabin nearly covered in vines and found scattered volumes of the *Encyclopaedia Britannica*, works by H.G. Wells and books on socialism. Near an old lineman's shack at Dare Point we happened upon a petroglyph figure carved in the soft rock below the tide line.

We hiked through a landscape drawing on the full palette of nature. Forest greens in a dozen hues, bone-white driftwood, frothy white breakers, sea green surge channels, powder blue skies, pink sunsets, jet black night skies with an infinity of twinkling stars. On the sandstone shelf we marvelled at potholes full of sea urchins, starfish, anemones, limpets and shiny black mussels. Near the mouth of the Cheewhat River Shelly stripped and dived in, catching a crab for dinner with her bare hands. We explored the sea caves at Owen Point and listened to the Pacific Ocean ricochet off the cliffs.

Although the last quarter mile through the forest seemed endless and we were covered in mosquito bites, we agreed the second trip had been incredibly satisfying. One more trip like that, we told ourselves, and we would probably stay in Port Renfrew forever.

The days were growing shorter, but the hikers continued to come. We estimated that 2,000 people had hiked the Trail that summer. The federal government was sending in a variety of scientists to check things out for the new park. There were several accidents, including a broken leg and a small forest fire which mobilized the BCFP crews. At last we realized the OFY cheques would soon cease; it was time to head back to the mainland. Shelly felt we were deserting the community, which had come to rely upon us to funnel the visitors onto the Trail with accurate information. We talked of coming back the next summer, but it was just talk. We said goodbye to our neighbours, packed up the Econoline van, and drove to Victoria.

What did we accomplish? We provided information to over a thousand parties, prepared a little guidebook for general distribution (it was followed shortly by a Sierra Club book), kept some people out of trouble both on the trail and in town, and set a precedent for an information centre at either end of the trail.

The West Coast Trail Information Centre project began as a kind of paid vacation, but it became the beginning of a longer journey. For me the experience led, like the logs across the forest floor, to a series of community-based jobs that sum up my various careers.

We acquired a fair bit of knowledge about the Trail, its history, its beauty and challenge. But we learned some other things as well. In the 1960s many young people were high on the idea of communities; some believed, like the anonymous builders at Tsusiat Falls, that communities could be created out of a little driftwood and sweat. Our stay in Port Renfrew taught us that even tiny communities are intricate and mysterious, not easily made or maintained. I think we were a little more humble for the experience.

Looking back from the vantage point of the 1990s and my own middle age, I can perhaps be excused for viewing the summer of '72 through a lens tinted ever so faintly with nostalgia. It is not only for my own lost youth, but for a brief season when all humanity seemed to experience a flowering of its more constructive impulses, a time when leaders could respond to the challenge of displaced youth – not by building relief camps or bolstering police forces, but by paying them to go out and search for new roles befitting a new age. ❖

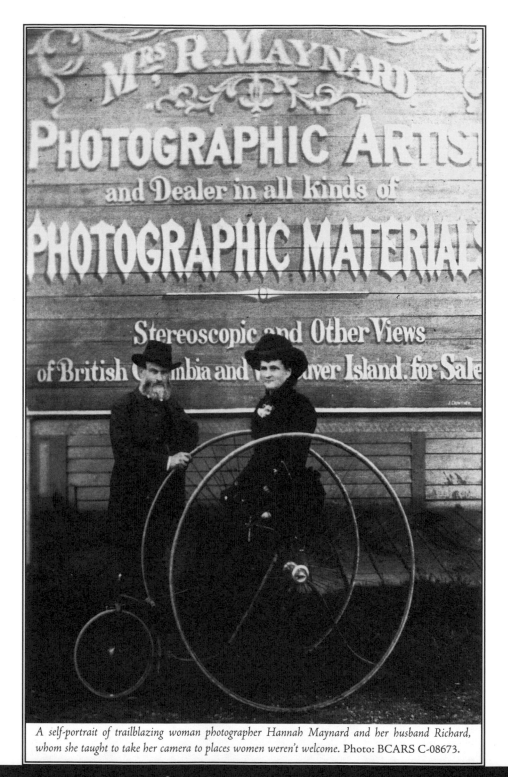

A self-portrait of trailblazing woman photographer Hannah Maynard and her husband Richard, whom she taught to take her camera to places women weren't welcome. Photo: BCARS C-08673.

Hannah Maynard:
Pioneer British Columbia Photographer

BY PETRA WATSON

By the 1860s, Victoria had changed from a hastily constructed fort serving the fur trade of the Hudson's Bay Company, to a busy port city and the centre of administration for the new colony of British Columbia. Lumbering and farming replaced fur exporting as the sustaining commercial activity in the area, and numerous businesses were established to serve local settlers, miners and fortune-seekers en route to the gold fields.

During the latter part of the nineteenth century, it was considered fashionable by the diverse and rapidly growing population of Victoria to visit the portrait studios of the city's professional photographers. One of them was Hannah Maynard. An anomaly as a professional woman photographer, Maynard ran "Mrs. R. Maynard's Photographic Gallery," a very successful studio practice in Victoria, from 1862 to 1912.

Hannah Maynard was born Hannah Hatherly in 1834 in Cornwall, England, and emigrated to Canada with her husband Richard James Maynard in 1852. They first settled in Bowmanville, Ontario where four of their five children were born: George, Zela, Albert and Emma. Their youngest daughter, Lillie, was born in Victoria. In 1859, Richard Maynard, a bootmaker by trade, travelled west to seek gold in the shallows of the Fraser River in southern British Columbia. After a brief but apparently successful sojourn, Richard returned to his family in Ontario. During his absence, Hannah had learned the techniques of photography.

The family moved to Victoria in 1862, and soon after, Hannah set up her first portrait studio on Johnson Street at Douglas. Richard Maynard spent that first summer placer mining for gold on the Stikine River – again, it is thought, with some success. On his return, he opened a boot and shoe store on Douglas Street near Johnson, and in 1874 Hannah moved her studio to the same building. Not long after, Richard learned photography, probably from Hannah. He was soon recognized as an excellent landscape photographer and was hired to document government-sponsored survey expeditions to northern British Columbia. The Maynards opened their third photography studio in 1892, on the upper floor of a two-storey brick building which they built on Pandora Avenue. (This building is still standing.)

Most of Maynard's clients were members of the burgeoning middle class in Victoria, and many of them made several visits to her studio. They wanted to be portrayed solemnly in photographs that would demonstrate social standing and economic prosperity.

Hannah Maynard's studio, in keeping with the traditions of nineteenth-century photographic portraiture, was a decorative parlour designed to make the most respectable people feel at home. Painted scenic backdrops, or decorative interiors almost rococo in design, created the portrait environment. Carved pedestals, diminutive fancy tables and ornate chairs were popular studio accessories. These props recalled the aestheticized tableau of the traditional easel painting, and in addition served as support structures that helped the client hold the pose without moving during the long exposure time. The painted backdrop of a landscape or a generously appointed salon was an environment suitable for showing off the elaborate fashions of the Victorian era.

The subjects of Maynard's photographic portraits – many of them middle- and upper-class men, women and children who often made consecutive visits to her studio – have remarkable physical and psychological presence. The affected poses and the self-conscious expressions so typical of nineteenth-century photography are in many portraits replaced by a feeling of ease, assurance and familiarity.

Maynard did not photograph only middle-class Victorians. She did portraits of sailors and other working-class people, and she invited Natives to the studio to be photographed in traditional dress – some of them wrapped in blankets and holding bundles of goods which they had brought to the city to sell.

Maynard also served as the official photographer for the Victoria Police Department between 1887 and 1892. Young boys, unusually stylish women and sullen men, most charged with theft or burglary, were walked from the police station, then along Cormorant Street to the Pandora Street studio for "mug shots." At first Maynard composed frontal full-face head and shoulder portraits, but later she experimented with a specially converted mirror that rested over the subject's shoulder and displayed both front and profile views in one image

"I think that I can say with every confidence," she is quoted as saying, "that we photographed everyone in the town at one time or another."

But Maynard did not limit her practice to the commercial portrait. She also undertook various forms of photographic experimentation – or as it was often called during the nineteenth century "photographic amusement." For example, she enjoyed producing composite photographs, or "Gems of British Columbia," made from the images of the many children Maynard photographed every year. It is thought that she composed the "Gems" from 1881 until at least 1894, and used them as studio promotion in the form of advertisements and seasonal greetings. To make them, she cut out and

pasted portrait photographs to a painted or photographed background, and then re-photographed the composition. "Gems" from previous years were incorporated in each new year's montage, creating a dense, visual display of tiny images of children. The "Gems," children as the jewels of nature, are steeped in both pathos and pleasure. They express youthful delight and comfort within the uncertainties and tragedies of childhood during the Victorian era, when diseases such as typhoid, diphtheria and tuberculosis were commonplace and usually fatal to young children.

During the late 1880s, Maynard also produced photographic images known as "statuette portraits." Described by her as "Living Statuary" and "Statuary from Life," these allegorical figures of pleasure, loss and despair appeared after a period of great sadness for Hannah: Lillie, her youngest daughter, contracted typhoid fever and died in 1883, at the age of sixteen. Maynard created a stat-

In addition to assiduously documenting daily Victorian life, Maynard was a tireless experimenter whose multiple exposure portraits display a wild sense of humour. Photo: BCARS F-05096.

uette portrait by placing the subject on a pedestal in front of a black background. To give a sculptural effect, the hair, face and/or other parts of the body were covered with white powder or rice flour. In the photograph, the figure of the body was dramatically visible against the dark background, and Maynard scraped or touched up the negative to heighten the cast-in-stone effect.

During the last few years, Maynard has become best known for the small number of double and multiple exposure self-portraits which she took during the 1880s. This form of experimentation, referred to as "freak" or "trick" photography, enjoyed a brief wave of popularity among professional photographers at the time. The photographer seeking information on multiple exposures could find numerous instructional articles in European and American scientific magazines and photographic journals such as *Scientific American* and the French journal *Nature*. The double exposure was the usual application, but Maynard undertook the more complex multiple exposures. Her technique was to protect part of the film with a lens cap or a box with sliding doors. (One simple attachment was made from a cigar box, cut down to size and blackened inside.) By arranging her subject and studio props strategically, and later touching up the negative to smooth out the joining of the different exposures, she created some unique images.

In her self-portraits Maynard manipulated the patterns of her domestic environment, turning a habitual action such as pouring tea, writing a letter or winding a skein of wool into playful, humorous scenes that are both fragmented and narrative.

The multiple exposure form is especially poignant here. Maynard was a successful professional woman with a large family, a situation fraught with powerful contradictions at the time, and her portraits evoke those contradictions – the warmth and comfort of domestic life, the social

Maynard photo of the Great War Canoe Race, a headline event at Victoria's annual regatta in the Gorge. Photo: BCARS A-02896.

"Gems of British Columbia," one of the strangely haunting photo-collages Maynard composed from her annual crop of children's portraits. Photo: BCARS F-05054.

norms of the Victorian middle class, the creative energy of her work, and the demand and responsibilities of being a wife, a mother and a photographer.

A selection of these double and multiple exposure photographs, said to be of the "freak order," were published in the journal *St. Louis and Canadian Photographer* in 1894.

These multiple exposure photographs have been regarded as Maynard's major body of work and have largely contributed to her reputation as a feminine "eccentric" of the Victorian era – a capricious and untimely woman. This attitude has mistakenly conferred amateur status on Maynard's photographic practice, and has exacerbated the lack of recognition of her professionalism, her success as a portrait photographer, and her contributions as a pioneer settler and a respected citizen of colonial Victoria. For Maynard, like other professional studio photographers of the late nineteenth century, artistic and technical experiments were only brief explorations, not the focus of her work.

Hannah Maynard travelled extensively throughout British Columbia, alone or with Richard. A correspondent from Seattle's *Weekly*

Pacific Tribune, visiting Victoria in 1878, stopped at Maynard's studio and learned that "she was on the upper Fraser and Cariboo road taking views." In August 1879, Richard and Hannah travelled together on a steamer around Vancouver Island. Richard often travelled alone on important commissions, such as accompanying the Indian Commissioner, Israel Powell, as far North as the Bering Sea in 1892 to undertake photographic work on the Seal Islands. But Hannah accompanied him on many trips and travelled on her own as well. Both the Maynards photographed landscapes, native villages and early northern white settlements, so the authorship of some images remains unclear. But collaborative photography was quite usual, so the photographs could be published during the late nineteenth century under either of their names. Also, as a woman photographer Hannah might have used Richard's name until her studio practice was established in Victoria.

Hannah Maynard's favourite outlet for publishing her own work, and sometimes that of Richard's, was the *St. Louis and Canadian Photographer*. In the September 1879 issue, the *St.*

Hannah Maynard travelled extensively throughout British Columbia, alone or with her husband Richard. Shown here, Richard Maynard poses in front of totems at Masset in the Queen Charlotte Islands. Photo: BCARS D-09210.

Louis Practical Photographer referred to Hannah Maynard as "one of the most industrious and preserving ladies we have in our business. She stops at no impediment, in our Art, but is a regular go-ahead, even beating our Yankee girls two to one in photography." On her retirement at seventy-eight, after fifty years of photographic practice, she was interviewed by the *Victoria Daily Colonist*, which reported: "Until the current year she never experienced a day's illness in her life. She [was] not tired of work or study… but she fancies that having worked for so long it is about time she made way for the younger generation." Hannah Maynard died in 1918 at eighty-four. ❖

Hannah Maynard travelled extensively throughout British Columbia, alone or with her husband Richard. Here she poses in front of totems at Skidegate on the Queen Charlotte Islands. Photo: BCARS G00822.

Illustration by Alistair Anderson

Donkey Boiler Coffee

BY ARTHUR "BILL" MAYSE

It was good coffee. A man with big feet could walk on it. It was the best coffee I ever tasted in my life, even if you did have to fish bits of burnt twig and charcoal out of it every now and then. But it had a taste, I think maybe from the quick, really savage boil in the white hot steam, that no other coffee anywhere else ever got, so we loved it.

Around about eleven o'clock in the morning when you were all tired out, ready for your break, you began to think about your lunch and, even more than your lunch, you thought about your coffee. Loggers' coffee in those days wasn't made on a stove at all and wasn't put in a thermos. They made it in the firebox of the donkey engine. The firebox is where they would have a roaring fire to keep steam in the boiler, because everything ran by steam in those years.

The loggers would be waiting and waiting and waiting, and then 11:30 finally came and the engineer would blow his whistle; he would go *woooo woo*—one long and one short—and that meant lunch time. So everybody would drop their gloves and head to the donkey engine.

As soon as that whistle blew the fireman, whose job it was to stoke the fires, would start making the coffee. On the donkey engine deck he would have an old soup box or a big milk container. In it he'd store a big bag of coffee and a lot of half-pound tobacco tins for the loggers to drink their coffee from, we didn't have cups.

He would take a great big lard pail, one of the great big storage pails that holds two or three gallons of water, off a hook and he'd reach for what he called his injector hose. This is one of the hoses that had hot, hot steam from the donkey boiler. He'd put some spring water in his bucket first and he'd take the injector hose and woosh, he'd send a big jet of hot steam into it and it would bring it right from cold to boiling in nothing flat.

Then the important thing, he'd take about two pounds of coffee, which is quite a lot of coffee, and he'd dump it into this furiously boiling water. Then he'd take what they called the slice bar, one of the steel pokers that they used for poking up the fire in the firebox, and he'd hang his pail with his coffee makings on one end of the slice bar and he'd ram it right into the white hot donkey boiler.

In a second it would be blowing steam all over the place, it boiled so quickly. He'd hold it there for a while and let it have a good bubble, good boil. The heat was terrible, his face would be all screwed up from the heat. Then he'd set the pail on the donkey deck and he'd grab another of these bags of cold water, drinking water, and he'd pour about two quarts into the coffee; that was to settle it down. And then the coffee was ready for drinking.

The fellows would all swarm on the donkey engine and grab the empty tobacco cans and they'd take a dip into the big steaming bucket of coffee and get a half-pound can of coffee, which is quite a lot. And there'd be canned milk, "canned cow" we called it, and sugar in bags and we'd fix our coffee the way we wanted it. I liked mine quite sweet without very much milk in it.

Then we'd all sit with our lunches—we brought our lunches from camp if we were working out on a job. We called them "nose bags" because they were a brown paper bag with, oh, about four sandwiches in it, four big heavy sandwiches made of some meat or other, whatever was going in camp. And there'd be a great big piece of pie, about a quarter of an apple pie. That would be your dessert and a couple of jam sandwiches and some cookies. That made a pretty hefty lunch but we were hungry.

We'd been working hard all morning so we were ready to eat. We'd open our lunch bags and start in on our sandwiches and then we'd reach for our coffee and nothing tasted as good as that first drink of what we called donkey boiler coffee after a hard morning's work.

While we were eating, the big ravens that come around every logging operation in the woods, would come looking for food and we'd throw them scraps of our sandwiches. Everyone was quite relaxed and happy. And we'd have maybe a refill of coffee and some fellows would even have two refills of coffee. I'd give a lot for a can of it right now. ❖

Few Native villages escaped the smallpox plague, least of all those like Alert Bay (above), situated along the major trade routes. Photo: BCARS D-04293.

The Great Pox

BY DOUGLAS HAMILTON

On March 22, 1862 an inconspicuous notice appeared in the Victoria *British Colonist*. A resident of New Westminster, recently returned from San Francisco by steamer, had come down with variola, or smallpox. Fortunately, the paper reported, "the case is not considered serious." These words were to herald in the worst recorded disaster ever to strike British Columbia. By the time it was over, the smallpox epidemic of 1862 had claimed the lives of one-third of BC's Native people – at least 20,000 of an estimated population of 60,000 – and a few dozen white people as well.

Before the arrival of the white man, the population density of Natives on the West Coast was greater than anywhere on the continent. Most of them lived in what is today BC, where a benign climate and abundant local food supported large populations. We do not know exactly how many people lived on the BC coast before the first censuses were organized in the 1880s. Newspapers of the 1860s

often quoted a pre-conquest figure of 35,000, but over the years we have learned the population was at least 100,000. White settlers underestimated the size of the Native population, possibly because it was easier, morally and legally, to take land from a few disparate people than from a large, recognized tribal group. In any case, official Canadian census figures show that by 1885, only 28,000 Natives were living in BC. A deadly combination of alcohol, firearms and previously unknown diseases devastated aboriginal people during the first century after contact, and the numbers did not begin to rebound until the 1920s.

Of all of the white man's terrible diseases, smallpox was the most destructive. No written records were kept by traders, miners or Natives, so the full extent of the catastrophe will never be known. But we do know that the smallpox epidemic was a watershed in British Columbia history. The sudden ravages of the disease effectively subdued

The sudden ravages of the disease effectively subdued the people of the First Nations like these near Cape Caution. Photo: BCARS D-08825.

the people of the First Nations and opened the door wide for conquest and settlement. The province of British Columbia would likely look very different today, but for one of earth's smallest and simplest life forms.

The little town of Fort Victoria was experiencing some growing pains in the early 1860s. It had been founded as a Hudson's Bay Company (HBC) trading post in 1843, and in 1851 Vancouver Island had become a Crown colony with HBC Factor James Douglas serving as governor. The town was populated by pioneer European immigrants and the local Natives who greatly outnumbered them. Trade between the two groups had prospered since the Europeans had first arrived, and in the spring of 1850 they had signed nine treaties, the Natives trading land for goods with the understanding that "our Village Sites and Enclosed Fields are to be kept for our own use, for the use of our children, and for those who may follow after us ..." One of these vil-

lage sites became the Songhees Reserve in the heart of Fort Victoria. Aboriginal people from many other groups travelled long distances to trade in Fort Victoria, and the gold rush of the late 1850s brought tens of thousands more white immigrants into town.

In a very short time Victoria grew to a bustling 5,000 with a hastily erected commercial hub of houses, tents, stores and warehouses. By spring 1859 more than 2,000 Natives were encamped within 200 yards of the fort and several hundred more were visiting at the Songhees reserve, including the warlike "Northern Indians" – Haida from the Queen Charlottes, Tsimshian from the northern mainland, and Kwakiutl from northern Vancouver Island. It was inevitable that whites and Natives would begin to clash over conflicting social values and over competition for parcels of land. And, with a growing concentration of people and hundreds of ships putting in to the port each year,

Mass infection was followed by panic and flight, which generated fresh outbreaks hundreds of miles from the source. Villages like Bella Coola became charnel houses. Photo: BCARS A-03980.

Smallpox survivors aboard the gunboat HMS Boxer. Photo: BCARS F-05167.

it was also inevitable that smallpox, the great world traveller, would eventually make an appearance at Fort Victoria.

Toward the end of March 1862, rumors of the dread epidemic among the Natives began to surface. Amor De Cosmos, the eccentric, flamboyant editor of the *British Colonist*, was one of the first to realize that the crowded town could be a perfect springboard for the "loathsome disease" among the neighbouring Native population. He noted the unusual "susceptibility to contagion of Indians" and called for the establishment of a smallpox hospital. Already the disease was rumoured to have taken hold in the Songhees reserve, and Dr. J.S. Helmcken, the HBC physician, had been ordered to vaccinate thirty Indians.

It had long been known that among popula-

tions never exposed to smallpox, the mortality rate was high – sometimes over 90 percent. When variola arrived in the New World with the early explorers in the early 1500s, the devastation it caused shocked and horrified even the hardened conquistadors. Early outbreaks in Mexico, Peru, Spanish Hispaniola, Cuba and Puerto Rico destroyed 50 to 90 percent of the Indians. Hernando Cortez's victorious march to the Aztec capital Tenochtitlán in 1520 was preceded and made possible by a crushing epidemic which eventually killed as many as half of Mexico's 30 million people. In his book *Of Plymouth Plantation 1620–1647*, William Bradford described the suffering of the Pequots in Connecticut: "For usually they that have this disease have them in abundance, and for want of bedding and linen and other helps they fall into a lamentable condition as they lie on their hard mats, the pox breaking and mattering and running one into the other, their skin cleaving by reason thereof to the mats they lie on. When they turn them, a whole side will flay off at once as it were, and they will be all of a gore blood, most fearful to behold. And then being very sore, what with cold and other distempers, they die like rotten sheep."

Bradford did not exaggerate. Smallpox was one of the most feared diseases in the world, with good reason. At the onset, the victim developed a fever, splitting headache and knifing pain in the back. A cough and runny nose developed. At this time the disease was difficult to diagnose because the symptoms were like those of many minor diseases, but those first days were the period of greatest contagion. Anything touched by the patient or his bodily fluids received a deadly dusting of viral particles. A single infected human lung cell could produce 10,000 to 100,000 seeds of death. On the second day the fever rose to 104°F. A terrible restlessness and sense of foreboding engulfed the victim, who was very sick indeed. If he was lucky, he slipped into a coma. Children often went into convulsions. On the third day a reprieve seemed to have been granted. The fever dropped and the patient felt a lot better – if he didn't know what he had. A mild rash began to show on his face. At this time the virus attacked the epithelial layers of the skin as well as the spleen, liver and other internal organs. On the fourth day the fever returned, and the victim's throat became terribly sore and his voice hoarse. The light pimply rash suddenly turned into hideous pus-filled pox wounds covering large areas of his face and neck. Thick scabs formed as if the victim had been badly burned, and in fatal cases there was extensive bleeding under the scabs which turned him black. The sores spread until they covered his legs, forearms and especially his back. As his face became swollen and distorted beyond recognition, the victim emitted a powerful stench. Severe sores in his mouth and throat made eating and talking impossible. Many victims in the last stages of the disease instinctively immersed themselves in water to quench the invisible fire. After the seventh day, the person began to die. If he survived

for two weeks, permanent immunity was assured. After a month or so, the scabs fell away and the sores began to heal, but the resulting scars would disfigure the entire body, especially the face and neck. The survivor was seriously weakened by the virus and vulnerable to a host of other opportune ailments such as skin infections, pneumonia, influenza and measles. Smallpox often attacked the eyes and was once the leading cause of blindness in the world. It also predisposed the survivor to arthritis, sterility and heart problems.

It is no wonder that panic began to spread among Native groups up and down the coast. At about the same time, reports surfaced that "vaccine scabs" were being sold among them. Scabs were carefully collected from smallpox victims, dried for several days or weeks and hawked for "two bits apiece." A scab was then bound into scarified skin on the arm of a healthy person. If the disease took, the arm became red and swollen and a low fever developed. With luck, the patient recovered in a few days and was immune to smallpox for life. No one knew why this kind of vaccination, or "variolation" as it was called, was effective (viruses were not even understood until 1907), but it had been used for centuries in Africa, India and China. In fact, the "advanced" countries of Europe were among the last to accept variolation.

The procedure was certainly not foolproof. Some 3 to 6 percent of those variolated, contracted the full-blown disease and died. There was the chance of accidentally spreading some other dangerous infection such as tuberculosis or syphilis. Also the smallpox virus remained extremely contagious, and new epidemics could easily be sparked off by those who had recently been variolated. They felt only a little under the weather, and went on travelling, trading and living pretty much as usual – scattering the deadly seeds of the virus everywhere they went. This was well understood at the time. At the height of the epidemic, the *Victoria Press* reported that one patient at the Indian hospital, a variolated woman, "will not keep to her room, but walks about and was even engaged in making bread for some 'tillicums' who if they do not come to grief after eating it, may certainly esteem themselves lucky." Informed observers knew that variolation had to be combined with some form of quarantine to keep the pox from spreading. Yet there is no evidence that anyone proposed large-scale variolation combined with quarantine as a remedy.

By the end of April, Dr. Helmcken had variolated 500 Natives in Victoria. But with a transient population of over 2,500 and no effective quarantine, the effect was minimal and the pestilence continued unabated. It quickly reached Fort Simpson, Fort Rupert and Nanaimo by ship and canoe. Reverend A.C. Garrett wrote to the *Colonist* of "fearful ravages at the Chimsean village" near Victoria. "Twenty have died within the past few days; four died yesterday, and one body lies unburied on the beach having no friends and the others are afraid to touch it. Those buried are only covered with two or three inches of dirt and it is feared that the disease will spread. Great alarm exists at the village, and it is thought that nearly the whole tribe will be swept away."

Two days later, on April 28, De Cosmos published a long and scathing editorial on the developing crisis. He predicted that the "savage occupants" of the local reserve "will rot and die with the most revolting disease that ever affected the human race." Chances were, he warned, "the pestilence will spread among our white population, a fit judgment for their intolerable wickedness in allowing such a nest of filth and crime to accumulate within sight of their houses, and within the hearing of our church bells." De Cosmos declared that the Indians should be evicted immediately, their village burned to ashes and their shallow graves thoroughly covered.

The Native exodus from Victoria began in late April 1862. For many it was voluntary. The Songhees, sensing the danger, packed up suddenly and left their reserve. The Tsimshians were given twenty-four hours to leave their encampment and a British gunboat took up a position across from the camp to "expedite their departure." The Commissioner of Police, Mr. Pemberton, began to evict Natives from Victoria. Roadblocks were erected, and the Tsimshian camp was "fired in the afternoon and every vestige destroyed."

On May 8, De Cosmos again demanded total and immediate expulsion of Native people, pointing out that the disease had spread to all the different tribal groups near town – Haidas, Tsimshians, Kwakiutl, Songhees, Stikeens. He sneered at the $100 which Governor Douglas had personally donated for relief of the Indians. "But what trifling it is with the lives of our own citizens to think private benevolence can afford the security for the public health that is demanded! or that it can prevent the Indians from rolling with the disease at our very doors."

But it was impossible to enforce evictions in unincorporated Victoria, where there no health or sanitation authorities and few police constables. And complete expulsion presented economic problems. Fort Victoria would be paralyzed without the Natives, who provided an indispensable labour force for the wheels of commerce. It was this labour force that probably received most of the variolations administered by Dr. Helmcken. But it was difficult to distinguish between the variolated and the unvariolated. And what about the Indian woman who had shared hearth and home with a white man for years and had borne his children? It was impossible to separate a mother from her children, and difficult to separate a man from his woman. Besides, if women and children were banished to the Indian camp, they could fall into a "state of moral corruption and turpitude ... under the skillful education of the red-skinned friends of their maternal relatives."

Only holy matrimony would make things right, argued the *Colonist*. Marriage would be "make the best of a bad bargain and honest women of their paramours at the same time." And their children could live "free from the taint of illegitimacy." But the notion that marriage and "legitimacy" would protect against smallpox was only a cover for a deeply held prejudice against the mixing of races. Many of the settlers believed the "purity and goodness" of the white race would be diluted in the children of mixed marriages. "The breed remains," Dr. Helmcken said of the Natives, "and will require a great deal of crossing to make a superior race." When the wholesale evictions at Fort Victoria soon proved unenforceable, and the colonial government issued special permits for Native mistresses, many whites were horrified at what they saw as a moral cave-in. The best they could hope for was that the Natives would eventually die out, or become assimilated into the white population. The vicious ravages of smallpox and other diseases could only bolster such hopes.

Indeed, the death rate among Natives rose rapidly. Dozens of new cases appeared daily, and by May 10, over 200 had died, 100 on the reserve and 100 on islands in the Canal de Haro (Haro Strait). The northern Indians living on the reserve were given three days to leave, and when they ignored the order, "fire was resorted to for the purpose of compelling them to evacuate, which they prepared to do yesterday afternoon after their houses had been leveled to the ground." Whites were forbidden entry into the deserted reserve. Even at this advanced date there were no white people with the virus in town, and only one in the hospital.

After the last encampment had been deserted, some voices at last began to be heard criticizing the colonial government for inaction during the crisis. Two smallpox hospitals had been established, one for Natives and the other for whites, but the former provided no real remedy to the Indians. The *Colonist* reported: "Indeed, the hospital, so called, is only a place where the victims may die in a heap without being obnoxious to anyone,

Native cleaning woman employed by pioneer photographer Hannah Maynard. Victorians' reliance on Indian labour was one reason officials were reluctant to enforce quarantine when it might have done some good. Photo: BCARS D-04293.

and not where they may obtain relief and attention as its name implies." The total number of variolations outside the white community remained pitifully small – probably less then 6,000 in all of BC – and not all of these would have taken.

Another delicate question arose: what had the Indian missionary societies done to stem the disaster? From the beginning of the British missionary movement in the late eighteenth century, trade, commerce, and money had been emphasized as much as religion. The missionary societies were a valuable tool for Britain in capturing and taming the far-flung outposts of empire. But the clergy was completely unprepared for the scourge of smallpox in BC. The chaos and turmoil of the epidemic, combined with mass evictions, undermined the entire missionary effort. With classrooms empty, almost all the money remained unspent. The local newspapers began to question the missions' inaction. "What were our philanthropists about," De Cosmos wrote, "that they were not up the coast ahead of the disease two months ago, engaged in vaccinating the poor wretches who have since fallen victims."

Meanwhile, the mass expulsions had the effect of spreading the virus everywhere along the coast. Smallpox was among the most stable of viruses, able to lie in a state of suspended animation for weeks, months, possibly even years without damage, and with an incubation period of eight to fourteen days it was perfectly adapted to wreak maximum havoc among a displaced refugee population. Almost all who opened their doors to the fugitives welcomed a killer. Mass infection was followed by panic and flight, which generated fresh outbreaks as far as hundreds of miles from the source. The villages, forts and islands between Victoria and Alaska became charnel houses.

Reports from ships' captains were published in the newspapers: "The ravages of small pox at Rupert has been frightful. The tribe native to that section was nearly exterminated. Forty out of sixty Hydahs who left Victoria for the North about one month ago, had died. The sick and dead with their canoes, blankets, guns, etc. were left along the coast. In one encampment, about twelve miles above Nanaimo, Capt. Osgood counted twelve dead Indians – the bodies festering in the noonday sun" (*Colonist*, June 21). "Capt. Whitford, while on his passage from Stickeen to this city, counted over 100 bodies of Indians who had died from the small pox between Kefeaux and Nanaimo. In some instances, attempts had been made by the survivors to burn the dead, by heaping brush over their remains and setting it on fire. It had partially failed in most instances, and fuel had burned out leaving the blackened, roasted bodies to rot, and pollute the air with overpowering exudations" (*Colonist*, July 7). "Lo! the poor Indian – Capt. Shaff, of the schooner *Nonpareil*, informed us that the Indians recently sent North from here are dying very fast. 80 or so pustules appear upon an occupant of one of the canoes, he is put ashore; a small piece of muslin, to serve as a tent is raised over him, a small allowance of bread, fish, and water doled out and he is left alone to die" (*Colonist*, June 14).

In Nanaimo, Anglican minister J.B. Good and the Vancouver Island Coal Mining and Land Company (VCML) worked together to variolate the Indians in the town's reserve – many of whom were employed by the company. Plans were also made to remove the Natives to a camp outside town limits on the Nanaimo River – ostensibly to lower the risk of disease for all, but as it happened, the VCML coveted the reserve land for a deep-water

wharf. At New Westminster, the Catholic priest embarked on an intensive one-man variolation campaign. When he claimed to have variolated over 1,000 Natives in one day, an indignant citizen wrote to the *British Columbian*: "The vaccination [variolation] of a thousand Indians in one day, and by one man, needs no analysis to expose its absurdity. I abhor alike that sectional jealousy which sees good only in its own, and that fervor which elevates men at the expense of truth."

The virus moved quickly up the Fraser, Nass and Skeena river systems. It spread from Bella Coola to devastate the Chilcotins, then it attacked the Southern Carriers along the West Road (Blackwater) and Chilako rivers in the fall of 1862. From the panic-stricken Carriers, it passed to the residents of Uncho, Tatuk, Cheslatta and Eutsk Lakes. "At first corpses were hurriedly buried in the fireplaces, where the ground was free of snow and frost. Then survivors contented themselves with throwing down trees on them; but soon the dead had to be left where they fell, and the natives still relate in their picturesque language that grouse used to do their wooing on the frozen breasts of human corpses."

Among the fishing camps of the Shuswap along the Fraser River, smallpox spread like wildfire during the August salmon run and then hitched a ride home with the participants. Prospectors from the North Thompson reported, "There are no Indians on the North River, as they nearly all died of smallpox this year." Whole communities were virtually annihilated by the disease, and some bands lost so many of their members, they joined other groups to survive.

Much farther to the north, William Duncan, that towering figure in British Columbia's missionary history, moved his flock of 400 Tsimshians away from Fort Simpson to nearby Metlakatla in July 1862, to protect them from disease and keep them away from the evil influences of the trading post. The timing was perfect. Duncan variolated his charges and the isolation served as quarantine – with spectacular results. Only five of his followers died, while a hundred times that number perished at Fort Simpson. Events at Metlakatla serve as an example of what could have happened, had the colonial authorities combined forces and acted promptly and responsibly.

The short- and long-term effects of the small-pox epidemic on BC's Native population cannot be overestimated. At least 20,000 people were killed outright, and most of the rest were seriously weakened, some left blind and sterile. Whole villages were wiped out or abandoned. Elderly people were most vulnerable to the disease, so keepers of tradition, oral history, and complex skills like carving and canoe-making died in disproportionate numbers. The elaborate ranking system of crests and clans was severely disrupted. The deaths of so many title holders meant that younger, less experienced men suddenly became heirs to the names, crests, songs and dances of their lineages. When several bands united for survival, whole new cultural systems had to be worked out. Shamans and medicine men were completely discredited, paving the way for the goals of the missionaries. The social order in many groups was seriously eroded, just at a time when it was most needed.

And there was a dramatic shift in the balance of power. Suddenly Natives found themselves strangers in their own land, marginalized by newcomers who could better resist European diseases. Growing opportunities in mining, logging and fishing drew even more white immigrants into the

Unable to cure smallpox, Native medicine men lost face before their own people. This Hannah Maynard photo of a shaman was taken at the Indian village at Hazelton. Photo: BCARS A-06031.

province. By 1885, the Native and white populations were about equal in size. "How have the mighty fallen!" De Cosmos wrote in the *Colonist*. "Four short years ago, numbering their braves by the thousands, they were the scourge and terror of the coast. Today, broken-spirited and effeminate, with scarce a corporal's guard of warriors remaining alive."

The smallpox epidemic also helped discourage the signing of any treaties between the Natives and the new settlers for many years. After the fourteen treaties Douglas arranged in the early 1850s, there were no more between the Crown and BC's Natives except for a minor one in the Peace River district in 1898. The ravages of the disease only strengthened whites' assumption that the Indians were a doomed race – accounts of the time refer to the extinction of the Natives almost as if it had already occurred – and if the Indians were all going to die out anyway, why bother signing treaties with them? The land was simply taken over by the Crown and passed on to white settlers. In the minds of many Europeans, the demographic disaster not only showed "God's anger" toward the heathen, it also provided vast lands for settlement, concrete evidence of God's good will toward the new Christian order.

There were complex reasons why white settlers in British Columbia were so unresponsive to the crisis, why whites were systematically variolated and quarantined while Natives were driven off, sometimes at gunpoint, to die by the tens of thousands. In the 1990s it may be easy to pass judgment, but a hundred years ago the authorities faced serious obstacles when dealing with the smallpox catastrophe.

Both of their two best weapons, variolation and quarantine, were regarded with fear and loathing by the Indians. Variolation killed a few of those who received it and often set off new outbreaks of smallpox. And because sores and skin rashes tend to look very similar, patients were accidentally variolated with syphilis, staphylococcus or tuberculosis. Variolation bore no resemblance to any Native healing practice of the day. Pressing a filthy scab into one's clean open wound must have seemed a barbarous and blasphemous act to those unacquainted with the treatment. Understandably, many Natives hid from the authorities, believing that variolation was a plot designed to spread the disease, not prevent it. Even when variolation was accepted, it was not effective without quarantine, which must have seemed a particular purgatory, to be avoided at all costs. For the whites who understood its purpose and value, quarantine worked very well. To the Natives, a place like the Indian smallpox hospital was a cruel prison filled with dead and dying people.

Another obstacle was the sheer speed and violence with which variola invaded a community. It struck without warning, and within two weeks virtually everyone in the village was either sick or dead. No prompt communication was available at that time, so it was impossible to co-ordinate an adequate defence. The chain of infection would burn itself out and move on, long before help could even be summoned.

But the strongest impediment to anyone wishing to stop the epidemic was the British colonial attitude toward public health. Today's view that promoting public health works for the common good was not a widespread belief in nineteenth-century England. Epidemics and plagues were seen as cleansing acts of God, both at home and abroad. For the powerful clergy, variolation and any inoculation were seen as direct interference with the plans of the Almighty. And "survival of the fittest"

was not just a figure of speech. England was a class-driven society much preoccupied with the "problem" of her own rapidly growing poorer classes. Thomas Malthus's *Essays on the Principles of Population*, which starkly laid out the frightening effects of overpopulation, was published in 1826. In it, Malthus offered a coolly logical solution to the problem: "Instead of recommending cleanliness to the poor we should encourage contrary habits. In our towns we should make the street narrower, crowd more people into the houses, and court the return of the plague. In the country, we should build our villages near stagnant pools, and particularly encourage settlements in all marshy and unwholesome situations. But above all, we should reprobate specific remedies for ravaging diseases, and those benevolent, but much mistaken men, who have thought they were doing a service to mankind by projecting schemes for the total extirpation of particular disorders." Malthus's views were in tune with the widely held beliefs of the time. If the poor in one's own country were seen as a disposable burden, the aborigines of conquered lands would be even more expendable. No wonder Britain was one of the very last "modern" countries to wholeheartedly accept either variolation or the cowpox vaccination.

Dr. Edward Jenner had published his groundbreaking *An Inquery into the Causes and Effects of the Variolae Vaccine* in London in 1798, presenting the first effective smallpox remedy that would almost never kill, and never spark off a new epidemic. Lymph from an infected bovine's running cowpox sore was rubbed into a person's cut skin and the mild disease, closely related to smallpox, gave immunity for about ten years. Cowpox could also be cultured using human subjects. Collecting and storing the infectious fluid was problematic in the mid-nineteenth century. It was easy to make the mistake of collecting fluids from sores that had nothing to do with the pox, but that were still deadly. Mysterious outbreaks of other infections were quickly traced to the practice, and questions of safety were raised. Moreover, to be effective the viral serum had to be collected at just the right time during its ten-day cycle of infection. And vaccination had to be repeated carefully every decade.

Still, many English people rushed to try the new vaccination during a smallpox outbreak in London in 1821. And other countries were quick to realize the benefits of it. US President Thomas Jefferson vaccinated his own large household in 1801 and distributed the first cowpox vaccine to local Natives a year later. The vaccination of Indians was provided for by an Act of Congress in 1832. King Carlos of Spain sent cowpox to his possessions in the New World in 1804, and Dr. Francisco Xavier de Balmis, the Johnny Appleseed of cowpox, stopped off at Puerto Rico, Cuba, Venezuela, Mexico, Peru and the Philippines, saving tens of thousands of lives. To keep the delicate virus alive, groups of indigent children were collected from local poorhouses in ports of call, and a few were inoculated every ten days during the long sea trip.

In Britain the story was quite different. Parliament passed laws making cowpox vaccination compulsory in 1841, 1853 and 1867, but no money was provided to enforce the acts until 1871, when dramatic events finally proved the value of inoculation beyond all doubt. During the grinding Franco-Prussian War in 1870–71, the inoculated German army lost only a handful of men to smallpox, while 21,000 non-inoculated French soldiers died of the disease. A new smallpox pandemic sparked by the French outbreak spread throughout Europe during 1870–75, killing half a million people.

All of these factors, combined with the HBC's emphasis on profit and indifference to social welfare, would have discouraged any public health crusader in Fort Victoria in 1862. But the administrators of the colonies of Vancouver Island and British Columbia could and should have done much more to contain the smallpox outbreak.

For one thing, large-scale inoculation would have been possible. The safe and effective cowpox vaccine was available from San Francisco within three days by express steamer. It was widely known that the vaccine had been used successfully elsewhere – several letters were published in the local papers to that effect – yet apparently no public official or enterprising entrepreneur considered offering the vaccine, even to Victoria's well-to-do white residents.

Teaching people simple hygiene for smallpox would also have been a cost-effective means of slowing the pestilence. If bodies of victims and their personal effects had been immediately disposed of, lives could have been saved. If the sick had been forbidden to travel instead of being forcibly evicted, many more lives might have been saved. And some rudimentary form of quarantine could have been enforced.

Fears of a runaway epidemic in white Victoria were completely groundless: natural immunity, variolation and quarantine insured that the virus would never gain a foothold. But instead of reassuring white residents and caring for aboriginal ones, the authorities allowed ignorance and yellow journalism to shift the public focus away from disease control and toward panicky self-preservation. Not only did the Indian victims of smallpox die in massive numbers, they also came to be blamed for causing the problem in the first place.

The terrible epidemic of 1862 was in fact the last of three smallpox epidemics that swept through the northwest coast between 1770 and 1862. The first arrived several years before the European explorers. Captain Vancouver noticed the telltale scars during his first circumnavigation of Vancouver Island in 1792. One of the earliest traders in sea otter skins, Captain Nathanial Portlock, stopped by Prince William's Sound in 1786 and observed: "The captain expected to have seen a numerous tribe, and was quite surprised to find only three men and three women, the same number of girls, and two boys about 12 years old and two infants. The oldest of the men was very much marked with the smallpox; as was a girl who appeared to be about fourteen years old. The old man endeavored to describe the excessive torments he endured whilst he was afflicted with the disorder which marked his face, and gave Captain Portlock to understand that it happened some years ago; he said the distemper carried off great numbers of the inhabitants, and that himself had lost ten children by it ... As none of the children under ten to twelve years of age were marked, there is great reason to suppose the disorder raged but little more than that number of years [ago]." In 1829, the American missionary Jonathan Green reported that about thirty years before, "the smallpox made great ravages" among the Haida. "This disease they call Tom Dyer, as some supposed from a sailor of the name who introduced it, through it is probable it came across the continent. Many of their old men recollect it, and they say, that it almost decimated the country."

The death toll of the first disaster is impossible to count, but calculating on the basis of other statistics in the New World, where Natives had no natural immunity, we can assume at least one-third of the people were killed. It is possible that the disease was brought by early undocumented visits from Europeans, but a more likely explanation lies to the south. In the 1770s a huge smallpox epidemic exploded throughout the western half of North America. The disease struck the Indians of the Missouri Basin and swept rapidly westward through the Dakotas, across the Rockies and up and down the Pacific coast. Annual migration patterns, and age-old trading routes for dentalium, abalone shell, slaves and other items, insured that the virus was spread far and wide.

The second great pox epidemic to lay waste to the northwest coast ran from 1835 to 1838. There are no documents on the event from BC, but farther north in Alaska, imperial Russia ruled the trade routes and careful records were kept. Smallpox was brought by the Tlingits to Sitka in November 1835. It spread like wildfire south to California, and north up the Principe Channel, to Norton Sound, the Aleutian Islands, Kodiak Island, the Alexander Archipelago, Fort Simpson and the Queen Charlotte Islands. The HBC in the south made almost no attempt to variolate, but Russia made vigorous attempts to arrest the epidemic in 1835.

The autocratic Tsars were among the first heads of state to endorse Jenner's revolutionary cowpox inoculation. Long before the vaccine became standard practice in England, Russian Indians were receiving it from St. Petersburg. Incredibly, the Russian Alaska Company's ship *Neva* brought the first cowpox inoculant to Sitka, Alaska in 1808. During the 1835 epidemic more than 4,000 inhabitants were vaccinated, most of them Russians, Creoles and Aleut hunters. But the rest of the Native population was widely dispersed, and most regarded the practice of cowpox vaccination with horror. Problems with shipping and storing the vaccinia also reduced the effectiveness of the Russian program. In the end, of an estimated 30,000 Eskimos, Haidas, Tlingits and Tsimshians, about 10,000 died, mostly because of the Natives' fears, technical problems with the vaccine, and communication shortcomings. Interestingly, the mortality rate in Alaska was about the same as that of the 1862 epidemic in BC – one-third of the total Native population.

So, if each of these three smallpox epidemics immediately killed off a third of the Indian population between California and Alaska, and if further tolls were taken by the fact that many survivors were rendered blind and sterile, and if other imported diseases such as whooping cough, measles, diphtheria, tuberculosis and syphilis killed even more Native people, the accumulated death toll is staggering. The pre-conquest Native population of British Columbia may have been much greater than the 100,000 figure often quoted by learned authorities.

The last case of smallpox in the wild appeared in 1977 in Somalia. Only two repositories now hold the living virus for "scientific study" – one in Atlanta, Georgia, and the other in Moscow, Russia. Mankind has been patting itself on the back for almost two decades over this remarkable feat of deliberate extinction. But all over the Third World, and particularly in Africa, shamans and medicine men still treasure and preserve pox dust (powdered scabs of smallpox victims) collected decades ago. Attempts by medical authorities to collect and destroy this almost magical powder have been to little avail. It was, after all, one of the few treatments used by early practitioners which actually worked. Is the monster just waiting for the right circumstances to strike again? If any of the pox dust were still infective, a whole new and terrible cycle could be sparked off – this time in a world that is completely unvaccinated. ❖

August Schnarr with a good catch of trout from the Homathko or Southgate River. Photo: Campbell River & District Museum #11642.

The August Schnarr Family of Bute Inlet

BY LYNN OVE MORTENSEN

Some folks who lived up the coast in the early years of the century might say that August Schnarr was a hard case. But those who know would say he just did what he had to do and, most of the time, did it well.

Schnarr was born August 29, 1886, after his folks came west from Kansas to homestead near Centralia, Washington. Three more children followed in quick succession. With all those mouths to feed, Schnarr's father turned to logging. He also drank, and when he'd been hitting the bottle, he was abusive.

In about 1900, when Schnarr was fourteen, the family left the homestead and moved to a small house on twenty-six acres near Chehalis.

That same year, Schnarr got fed up with his father's abuses. He and his twelve-year-old brother Gus jumped their father on his way home from a drunk, and told him to clear out. August took over and ran the family with a tight hand from then on. The area around Chehalis was big fir timber country and pioneer machinery was primitive. In those days, Schnarr recalled, "you had to work; nobody'd hand you anything. We just had axes, bucking saws – not very good ones – augers." To take down a big fir, folks would bore a hole 18 inches deep into the base above the roots. Then they'd angle in another hole to meet it, to provide a draft. They'd light a little pile of tinder where the holes met. The fire would smoulder and burn

41

DOUGLAS COLLEGE LIBRARY

for a while and "all of a sudden the tree would fall." First you cleared a little place for a garden, then enough ground for a cow.

August and his brothers cut cordwood and sold it for $3.50 a cord. They also hunted for meat, and their mother cooked and canned produce from their large garden. In 1905, Schnarr negotiated with a logging company to trade lumber for a rail right-of-way and the whole family worked together to build a large log house.

In 1907, when Schnarr was twenty-one, he got his first taste of British Columbia when he and Gus rowed up the coast, stopping at Gastown and Victoria. In June 1909, he and a friend hired on with a logging camp near Port Harvey on Cracroft Island. The mosquitoes, gnats and horseflies were so thick he remembered "you had to keep one hand going all the time."

He headed home to Chehalis when the camp closed for the winter but returned the following spring. With him aboard the old *Cassiar* this time

were his younger brothers Gus and Johnny, and a 16-foot double ender. The brothers were soon hooked on the coast and were determined to find work over the winter. At the end of the season, they rowed across Johnstone Strait and set a trapline near the Adams River.

That same winter (1911–12) August, Johnny and a friend set out to explore Bute Inlet. They watched local natives hewing out canoes and built one of their own in similar fashion. Then they headed up the Southgate River, trapping marten and some mink along the way, and camped at the head of the inlet near the entrance of the Homathko River.

In 1912, August, Gus and Johnny, along with Paddy McCallum, tried their own hands at logging flood-downed trees in the Adams River. They took out two or three sections over the summer. When fall arrived, the brothers headed back up Bute to build a cabin twenty miles up the Southgate. They trapped in Bute the next two winters, and in the

The Schnarr float house at Shoal Bay circa 1924. Photo: Campbell River & District Museum #14388.

summer they explored the area as far as Knight Inlet by rowboat and sail.

In 1914, Gus and Johnny both left the region but August's patterns were established: handlogging in summer, trapping during the winter, mostly up Bute, and picking up the odd dollar for the bounty on cougars. He was a loner, and he learned to fall all kinds of trees with a springpole. First he'd make an undercut. Then he'd man one end of the saw with a limber young tree tied to the other, carefully arranged to get just the right tension to make a level cut. This he preferred to a human partner. He was always careful about accidents and "couldn't work with a reckless man."

Schnarr appreciated his freedom. He liked the absence of regulations, being able to cut any tree or kill any animal he wanted. He trapped cougar with dogs and liked a dog that was fast. He had no use for hounds who might follow an old scent. He travelled "clean through the canyon to the interior" up both the Klinaklini and the Homathko rivers. He built shacks all the way through, always near fresh water and plenty of wood. "That was lovely, beautiful country, that Waddington Trail." In lots of places there was just one trail and he'd set traps on either side. Though it was common to trap marten inland and mink and sometimes otter on the waterfront, Schnarr mainly caught marten up Bute. He was proud to announce that "the North West Fur Company said I brought in more marten than any ten men."

In 1917, after the US entered World War One, Schnarr was drafted. He left a 30-foot canoe, several guns and his handlogging outfit with a fellow on Stuart Island to sell on commission and dutifully trooped south to join up. But home from the war, he found his possessions gone and the man uncommunicative. Schnarr was enraged. In later years he stated that he didn't like lying and swore he'd never cheated anyone. One of his mottos was: "Be in the right and have the determination to carry through." He liked to hold up a clenched fist and declare, "Ya see that? It never failed me." But for the moment, Schnarr had to start over.

He got a job in a small machine shop at Shoal Bay. One day he heard about a pretty young woman who had settled with her parents at Cameleon Harbour on Sonora Island. He went on over and met Zaida Lansell. They were married in 1922 and moved into a float house at Shoal Bay. That same year, baby Pansy was born in Zaida's parents' home in Cameleon Harbour.

One day in the store at Shoal Bay, Schnarr spotted the guy who was supposed to have sold his belongings. This time, he didn't let the fellow get away. Many years later Schnarr recounted the scene in a high, crackling voice punctuated by an occasional giggle. "Here's where we settle up," Schnarr said. "I shoved him back and landed one on him. I popped him one and down he went. Three times I knocked him down. And then I said, 'tell ya what. Every time I see you I'm gonna hit you.' Schnarr saw the guy twice more, once on the Union boat and again in a hardware store in Campbell River, but both times the culprit managed to get away before Schnarr could carry out his vow.

Two more girls, Pearl and Marian, were born in the hospital at Rock Bay while the family lived in Shoal Bay. Shortly after, probably in early 1926, Schnarr towed the float house up Bute and skidded it onto a homesite halfway between the Orford River and the head of the inlet. The site, which came to be called "Schnarr's Landing," was to be August's home base and emotional cornerstone on and off over the next forty years.

Pansy was nearing school age. Since Zaida insisted on schooling for her girls, in 1928 the blond six-year-old was sent to board with a Mrs. Brians for 18 dollars a month so she could attend the school in Shoal Bay. Mrs. Brians took her along to dances, where she'd be put to sleep tucked in behind the piano. Also, probably unknown to any of them, Zaida was entering the initial stages of a terminal illness.

By the following September, Pearl was also ready for school and the girls went to live with Mrs. Asman, who later became Mrs. Muehle, wife of the sheep farmer at Big Bay, Stuart Island. Pearl's memories of Big Bay days contribute added sparkle to the always-exciting images of Stuart Island fishing. She recalls natives from the Old Church House Village on Sonora riding the eddies in big old

Zaida Schnarr and daughters (left to right) Pansy, Pearl and Marion at Stuart Island in the early 1920s. Photo: Campbell River & District Museum #14409.

dugouts, the women glowing in brightly coloured satin evening gowns ordered from Simpson's or Eaton's catalogues.

At Big Bay, board rose to 20 dollars a month per child. In a time when the family income hovered around $3,000 a year, that was a large chunk, more than twice the monthly rent. Rent on the homesite lease in April 1929 was $8.50. A new Gilchrist jack cost about 35 dollars (though Schnarr preferred stronger, geared models made by Ellingsons), and a pair of Raintest pants went for $4.50. Schnarr picked up extra money trapping cougar and wolf. Cougar skins brought 10 dollars while briefly, in 1929, the bounty on cougar rose to 40 dollars.

The indomitable Schnarr didn't sit still for long. He guided survey parties, including a 1927 – 28 hydro exploration for power sources in the Bute/Chilcotin region. When, years later, the

W.A.C. Bennett Dam went through on the Peace River instead, Schnarr condemned it as a political plum. He felt there was more power potential in the Chilcotin and that a dam there would have caused less destruction of farmland and fish habitat.

Sometime during the twenties, he spent nights absorbing engineering theory and practice by the light of a coal oil lantern and earned an engineering diploma by correspondence. If he wanted something, he'd build it, including an unusual hand-hewn bathtub. He was practically penniless most of his life, yet he managed to build himself several rather exotic pieces of equipment, including an air-boat for travel up nearby rivers like the Homathko and Southgate, and an electromagnet for hauling boom chains.

In May 1932, in the depths of the Depression, Zaida died of cancer. She was only about thirty-one years old. Her body was carried to Cameleon

Harbour aboard the Columbia Coast Mission boat *Rendezvous* for a funeral service conducted by Reverend Alan Greene. The girls remember the last note Zaida wrote to them, using her left hand because she could no longer manage the right one.

To Pansy and Pearl, Zaida remains a dim presence since they spent so little of their childhood at home. They spent summers at the Bute homestead, but their memories are of playing in the water all day, coming in only to eat dinner and go to bed. Because of the dreaded "Bute wind," they remained on Stuart Island at Christmas when "Santa" Alan Greene would arrive, bearing oranges, candy and a small gift for each child.

Possibly because of Zaida's death, but also because Logan Schibler was trying to round up enough children for a school, Schnarr decided to move to Owen Bay. He skidded the house back onto a float and headed down the inlet, towing it with a little old Easthope. Generally, Schnarr liked to carry two small kicker engines aboard, so there would

At one time, August brought home four orphaned cougar kittens. Two died fairly quickly, but both a male and female survived to adulthood, bringing the girls a measure of notoriety when their unusual pets made international news. Photo: Campbell River & District Museum #15621.

In early 1926, Schnarr towed the float house up Bute and skidded it onto a homesite halfway between the Orford River and the head of the inlet. The site came to be called "Schnarr's Landing." Photo: Campbell River & District Museum #9005.

always be "one to come home on." But in this instance his precautions proved useless. Near Stuart Island a violent wind arose and Schnarr watched, helpless, as the float broke up and the house went to the bottom.

So he started over again. He and Logan Schibler tore apart buildings from an abandoned logging camp at Orford River, salvaging lumber, windows, bricks, even nails. Schnarr set the girls to straightening nails and, using all salvaged materials, whacked together a three-room shack over a cellar.

Various relatives came to watch the girls for a while but by the time Pansy reached age twelve, she took over running the household. It was "slim pickens," but they never went hungry. August shot deer and raised pigs; he made his own bacon and smoked fish. The family cultivated a huge garden and Pansy learned to can hundreds of quarts of meat, vegetables and fruit from the orchard each year. The only staples they bought were flour, oats, brown sugar, peanut butter and Pacific milk.

During the winter the girls attended the Owen Bay school, a small shack on floats. Daydreaming students could watch the water through cracks in the floor. But come summer, August dropped them at the old Bute homestead, sometimes for as long as six weeks. They lived in the only building left, an open boat shed, where they slept on straw, tended the garden and competed with local black bears for wild berries to can for winter. Schnarr treated them like boys, teaching them to hand log, bore boomsticks with an old crank auger, run the boats, even tend traplines.

Schnarr didn't believe in play, but one time, when Pansy was about thirteen, he brought home four orphaned cougar kittens. Two died fairly quickly, but both a male and female survived to adulthood, bringing the girls a measure of notoriety when their unusual pets made international news.

As the girls entered their teens, natural conflicts increased on the home front. August didn't approve

The Schnarr girls with their father. Photo: Campbell River & District Museum #15627.

of dances and feared his daughters' contact with young men in general. In 1936, he skidded the Owen Bay house back onto floats and towed it up Bute once more. Nevertheless, young men would sneak up the inlet to visit when August was away. At nineteen, Pansy "escaped" to a job in Sayward and married a childhood acquaintance shortly afterward. Her sisters followed suit, leaving August to fend for himself back at the Bute homestead, where he continued his familiar rounds of trapping and handlogging till the early sixties.

August Schnarr lived to be ninety-five. He spent his last years in a small home at Heriot Bay on Quadra Island. On a clear day he could see halfway up Bute from his living room window.

Pansy recalls her tough father with a touch of sympathy. "Everybody says how grumpy he was… but, you know… he lost his wife, he lost his house, left with three little girls, no money. It must have been very nerve-wracking for him… He had a pretty hard row to hoe.

"He liked the loneliness of Bute… The older he got, the more Bute belonged to him. So we took his ashes up there, we figured he would like that." ❖

August Schnarr with a cougar and neighbour, Mrs. Williams. Photo: Campbell River & District Museum #8493.

The Rock Bandits

BY PAUL LAWSON

Day after day,
hour after hour,
they grind away at their
unfinishable, unfathomable mission –
To make our world
a smaller place to live.

They are the rock bandits.
Those restless souls
who have come and gone
in search of their quarry.
Those dust eating deaf
who have lit the suffering fuse
and hidden from
the flyrock of life.

To places barren
they have gone
to reduce the magnificent
to mounds of rubble
All in the name of
some hangover thirst for
the nectar of the earth.

To places untravelled
they have travelled
so that others could
come that way
and marvel at their music
written boldly
on the faces
of those disappointed peaks

The powder that's gone
up in smoke
could fuel another war
or maybe it has already
fatalities by the hundreds,
death is a way of life –
All in the name
of flyrock and glory.

Some say the rock dust and nitro
makes them that way –
After conducting
a lifelong study
I'm here to say
that they're right

Those thirty-day headaches
just do something
to your attitude.

When will they stop
these raving rock bandits
from turning our
cordilleran home
into some piecemeal prairie
They've already made a good start –
flying time
has been notably reduced
by their air-tracked assault

It's a quest
that's insatiable,
an itch
that's unscratchable,
a disease of the heart
the only cure for which
is to push the fire button
on a regular basis

Perhaps we should
start a foundation
to find an exotic cure
for this deafening passion
While there's still some oceans
that haven't been filled in,
some mountains that
haven't yet succumbed
to the percussion section
of that orchestra of doom

I've got it under control
but there isn't
a Hallowe'en that goes by
where the smell of powder
doesn't catch my nostril –
and like some seagull circling
over a spawned-out salmon
the urge to return
overpowers,
and my thumb
begins to twitch
in anticipation ❖

Illustration by Alistair Anderson

The Deer???

BY DICK HAMMOND

Author's note: This story may be received with more skepticism than most, for the animal involved is familiar to people who live in the country as well as to many city dwellers and is not usually credited with uncommon intelligence. Therefore I thought it might be well to preface this story with a short account of a trick I saw used by a deer in the wild.

I was walking in the woods one autumn morning. The route led over a ridge of rock separating one small valley from another. The area had been logged not many years before, and most of each valley was visible from the ridge. It is my habit in such a case to crest the ridge as quietly as possible in the hope of seeing something interesting on the other side. In this instance I was able to walk more silently than usual as there were few bushes and the rocks were covered with soft moss damp with dew. A slight breeze was blowing across the ridge, so I knew that my scent wouldn't alert any animals in front of me. As soon as I could see into the valley beyond the ridge, I stopped to look around, and almost immediately saw a deer about fifty yards below and in front of me, nibbling at a clump of huckleberry bushes. It was nothing special, just a two-point buck of average size, but I enjoy watching animals in their natural state when they don't know they are being observed, so I stood very still, breathing as quietly as possible. (This may seem to be an unnecessary precaution, but anyone who has witnessed them in action knows what incredibly acute senses some wild animals have.)

The deer browsed a bit on the huckleberry shoots, took a few steps, nibbled at some other bush, moved on again. Its ears waggled now and then, and once it paused to scratch its shoulder with its hind leg. Its path took it towards and behind a fairly large fir tree – about four feet through – that had been used as a spar tree by the loggers. As the deer measured about five feet from nose to tail, one would expect its head to appear before its tail vanished. Only it didn't. Perhaps it had turned a bit to reach a tasty bush? I waited. No deer. I watched closely but saw no movement. Suddenly suspicious, I shifted a few feet to one side to get a better look. I saw the deer all right , but in

another few seconds I wouldn't have. It was just slipping into the fringe of brush on the other side of the valley, at least a hundred feet away from the fir tree! It had known exactly where I was, and had headed for the nearest cover keeping the tree between itself and me the whole while. Just imagine the skill required to do this while walking over ground littered with the debris of logging, and doing it with your back turned! I know that I couldn't have done it.

It might be objected that deer can quite often be observed acting in a manner that amply justifies the term "dumb animal." To this I can offer no explanation, but might mention that the area I was in had been heavily hunted for many years.

And now, on to the story.

The place, one of the inlets beyond Pender Harbour. I think it may have been Narrows Arm. Why they picked that particular valley, I don't know, but Father had promised to take his friend "Shorty" Roberts on a hunting trip, and this was the place they chose. Probably because neither of them had hunted there before, nor knew of anyone else who had.

They dropped anchor at a creek mouth, in a bay where the water was calm and sheltered. Though it was late in October and the weather stormy, they wouldn't have to worry about the boat.

Father looked around them as Shorty got into the skiff. The mountains were almost covered with clouds which came to within a few hundred feet above the water. There was almost an inch of snow at the beach, and the trees were more white than green. A few small flakes were drifting down. It would be hard, he thought to imagine a more gloomy prospect. Steep hills all around them, grey sky close above, snow.

Shorty was as excited as a hunting dog when its master takes the gun down.

"What a perfect day Hal! Just enough snow, and fresh too. Any tracks will be today's – we should have a great hunt!" He knew that Father was aware of all this, but his excitement had to have an outlet.

"Shorty wasn't much to look at," Father said, "but he was all heart and sinew. He could walk all day with his boots full of snow and his clothing wet and not seem to notice it. He never complained. He loved to hunt. I never saw a man that enjoyed hunting as much as Shorty did. He couldn't get enough hunting."

They rowed ashore, pulled the skiff above high tide level, and headed up the valley. It was quite steep at first, and hadn't been logged except for a few trees near the shore that had been taken out by handloggers. After a hundred yards or so, the slope became more gradual before rising into the foothills of the mountains. The small creek that drained the valley was chattering and gurgling not far away. They kept to the left side where a considerable area had been burned not long before. This would be the most likely place for deer, for they like to browse on the bushes that grow up in a burn and tend to avoid old-growth forest if possible, although they like to bed down on the edge of it.

The two hunters had scarcely entered the burned area when they heard the thump of hooves. The sound was of a heavy deer, and they both spotted it at the same time, a huge buck showing for a second or two between the clumps of young trees.

"Man oh man," breathed Shorty. "Did you see that rack of horns? There's our buck!"

A few moments, and they were looking at the tracks in the snow.

Shorty was awed. "Will you look at those tracks! That deer must go over two hundred pounds. We've just got to get him. Let's go."

They checked their rifles and began to follow the tracks. As they went along, they both scanned the country around them alertly. Sometimes a deer will stand and watch you from some vantage point, curious as to what might be following, especially in a place where they have seldom or never been hunted, such as this valley.

They walked steadily on, not making much effort to be silent, for they could never be silent enough that the deer wouldn't hear them. But suddenly there were no more tracks. They just came to an end halfway across a patch of clear ground. There was – at this height – about two inches of snow.

"He must have made a jump off to the side," said Shorty. "Let's circle."

They separated, each taking one half of a little circle around the point at which the tracks disappeared. But they found no tracks. Aroused now, they coursed the area checking for bare spots where the snow hadn't stayed, or anywhere that a track might be concealed. Nothing.

"Well," said Shorty. "I'm damned if I ever saw anything like this. What do you think of it Hal?"

Now Shorty was a good and enthusiastic hunter, with an average talent for observation, but Father was a superb tracker, by far the best I've ever known.

"I knew I hadn't missed anything," he told me, "and I was pretty sure the deer hadn't suddenly sprouted wings and flown away. There was only one thing left."

So he looked carefully at the tracks in the snow. It wasn't easy, as they had walked over most of them.

"Shorty," he called. "Come here and look at this."

Shorty came over to where Father was standing. "Look there. What do you think of that?"

Shorty looked at the track. Then he got down on his knees and poked at it gently with his finger. He rose to his feet. "That deer has walked backwards in his own tracks. I never even heard of a deer doing a thing like that."

"Neither have I. That must be some smart deer. Probably so old and tough you'd have to chew the gravy."

"Well," said Shorty, "let's backtrack and find where he cut off. Don't see how we missed that."

Back they went, walking slowly, looking carefully at each side of the line of tracks. After they had gone about a hundred feet, Father knelt and examined one of the tracks closely.

"We've missed it. This is a single print," he announced. "OK. You go up, I'll go down. We'll find the spot this time."

Now they walked about fifteen feet away from the line of tracks. They had gone some fifty feet when Shorty called, "Come here Hal."

As Father approached, Shorty pointed. There were the tracks they had been seeking, bunched closely together behind a little clump of brush, where they couldn't be seen from where the other tracks were. Father looked around. Then he walked further uphill to where a small tree had fallen.

Another set of bunched tracks was concealed behind it. They led along beside the tree, then angled off up the hillside.

He shook his head. "A deer that smart, a man could feel like a murderer shooting. But," he continued not fully convincing even himself, "nature is a wonderful thing, and instinct is sometimes just as good – or even better – than thinking. A deer is, after all, just a deer. A wild animal."

Shorty stood there looking serious. Finally he said, "Yeah, I suppose you're right. Let's go after him."

They followed the tracks, paralleling them now, not walking on them. Suddenly Father, who was leading the way, said, "Well I'll be darned. Look at that!"

They had come up to a bushy young fir tree about as tall as a man. The deer had gone behind it, then had turned around and faced back downhill.

"What's so funny about that?" asked Shorty. "He just turned around to see if we were coming after him."

"Look closer. He's been standing there for quite a while. I'd say for all the time we spent trying to find where he went. Just his head sticking out from behind this tree. He knew we couldn't see him, and he was curious. Those tracks are only seconds old. He started off again when he saw we had caught on to him. Not very fast either. He's not much afraid of us."

Shorty made no answer, which was strange for he had always some comment to make about everything.

"Let's go," said Father. "He can't be more than a couple of hundred feet ahead of us. We should be able to spot him in this burn."

But they didn't, and as they went on the reason became clear.

"That deer," he told me, "always managed to keep something between him and us. It was uncanny the way he did it. I know that at any time he was never too far away for us to see him, but we never did."

And now once again the tracks disappeared. Father had been expecting this to happen. He was sure the deer would try something else to throw them off the trail. They stopped where the tracks ceased and looked around them. Father knelt and examined the last few tracks.

"Nope," he announced, "he didn't backtrack this time. I didn't think he'd repeat himself. Let's start looking."

They circled the area, checking everything that could possibly conceal tracks. The ground was wet and soft, spotted with scattered outcrops of rock, most of which had no snow on them, as the ground water kept them just warm enough to melt it. Father passed near one of them, then turned back and looked at it more closely. He beckoned to Shorty and pointed to the rock. There was a small fragment of mud and snow on it.

"He's jumping from rock to rock," Shorty said, "using them as stepping stones." He looked around. "It's going to take us a long time to find which ones he's used."

"No," said Father. "I don't think we'll have to do that."

"Why not?"

"I think that deer is standing out there not far away, watching to see how long it takes us to find his trail again. Probably just over that ridge there. If we spread out a bit and move straight towards it we should jump him and maybe get a shot at him. What do you think?"

"I don't know what to think," replied Shorty slowly. "But I'm game to give it a try."

This didn't sound like the Shorty Roberts that Father knew. He looked sharply at his friend.

"His shoulders were all hunched up," Father said, "and there was no sparkle in his eyes. But I thought, 'He'll perk up when we spot that deer again.'"

So off they went, separating so as to approach the ridge from two different angles. Father whistled at Shorty, and pointed. There were the tracks, leading to just where he thought the deer would be. But they saw no deer. It had been there, and it had been watching them just as it had before, but once again it had slipped away as they approached, taking cover in such a way that they couldn't sight it.

"He's bound to slip up if he keeps on playing tricks like this," Father predicted confidently.

Off they went once more, the tracks leading them on, so easy to follow. The snow was falling faster now, but they could still see far enough ahead to shoot, if their quarry should happen to show himself. The trail led straight up the valley towards the unburned timber, and this time they walked for about fifteen minutes before the tracks came to an end.

Father knelt, looked closely. "Hasn't back-tracked." He walked downhill a bit, looked back. Shorty was standing there, rifle under his arm, shoulders in that uncharacteristic hunch, his hat and jacket powdered with snow, looking up the valley, making no effort to help find the trail. Father watched him for a moment but the puzzle was too intriguing to waste any time wondering about his partner's actions. He cast back and forth like a hunting dog, forward and back, uphill and down. There was no trace. This time the deer did indeed seem to have "sprouted wings and flown away." He went back to where Shorty was still standing.

He said, only half jokingly, "Two pairs of eyes are better than one you know."

"I think we should go home," Shorty replied. "It's too far to drag a big deer like that anyhow."

"Home?" repeated Father, incredulous. "Why, this is just getting interesting. What's the matter with you? How can you even think of going back without finding out what that deer has done this time to throw us off?"

"Hal," said his friend, more serious than Father could remember ever hearing him. "Have you ever heard of 'The-deer-that-is-not-a-deer'?"

"No, can't say as I have. How in heck can a deer be a deer and not a deer at the same time?"

"I just thought you might have. You know a lot of Indians. One of the old ones told me once that in some of the wild places like this valley, if a man is foolish enough to hunt there, he may meet the 'deer-that-is-not-a-deer.' It will lure him farther and farther into the mountains. If he keeps on after it, he's never seen again. You see, it's something more than a deer, though I don't know what. And this thing we're following sure as hell doesn't act like any deer I've ever hunted. It thinks like a man. It knows how we hunt, what we look for. How could a deer know that? And what good would these tricks be up against scent hunters, like wolves or cougars? It's not natural. Let's go back while we can go back."

Father thought for a moment. "Well, if you ask me, your critter is going to a lot of trouble to lose us if he wants us to follow him. A nice plain set of tracks would make more sense."

But Shorty had an answer to that. "If we'd had a nice plain set of tracks, we'd have given up and be heading back to the boat by now." He pointed up to the snow-covered trees dimly visible through the drifting flakes. "Would you follow a straight-line set of tracks up into that? Course you wouldn't. If you hadn't got a shot in by the time we got in there, you'd have turned around and gone home. But as it is now, you're hooked. You can't wait to find out what that thing did this time, and what it's going to do next. That's right isn't it?"

"I looked around," Father told me. "Everything was white or grey or dark green. The only sound was the hissing of the snow. You couldn't see more than a couple of hundred feet. I didn't believe a word of what Shorty said, but I thought suddenly of how the nearest other human was about thirty miles away by boat, how we might be the only people to ever walk into that valley, and in spite of myself, I felt something like a little cold shiver go through me. I had the feeling that we were at the end of the world, and there was no one else."

"Well Shorty," he said, "you know where the boat is. Go back there and wait for me. If I'm not back by dark, don't wait any longer. Something may come looking for you!"

He turned around and scanned the ground intently, trying to think of a way the deer could hide its tracks.

He noticed a little clump of salmonberry bushes about two feet high, and thought that bush should have more snow on it than that. So he went for a look, and sure enough, there were the tracks right in the centre of the clump. "I looked back at Shorty," he said, "and I thought, by Gad, if I was a superstitious man, I could believe there was something in his story at that." That deer had covered about twenty feet in a single jump and landed so as to have hardly disturbed that clump of bushes. It was marvellous!"

Now that he knew the way the deer had gone, he looked around to see where it could have gone next, and spotted a similar clump of browsed-down bushes about the same distance down the slope. When he reached it, there were the tracks in the middle of it. The only cover from there was a brush-covered little creek, but the snow was undisturbed on the bushes lining the bank. He walked slowly up and down examining every possible place where the tracks could be concealed, and finally he found them. They were just over the edge of where the bank sloped sharply down to the stream bed, out of sight unless you walked right along the bank. The deer must have gone into the brush here, even though the snow appeared undisturbed. He saw some odd marks on the ground.

"Shorty," he called. "Come down here and take a look at this."

All this time Shorty had stood unmoving where the tracks had stopped. Now he climbed down to where Father was.

"What do you make of that?" Father asked, pointing to the marks.

Shorty looked closely at the ground and then at the bushes.

"That deer got down on its knees and crawled under those bushes, and it didn't hardly knock off any snow doing it, in spite of carrying a rack of horns about a yard wide. Hal, do you still think that's just a deer you're following?"

"Yes, I do. A smart deer, the smartest deer I've ever hunted, but just a deer, and I'm going after him."

Shorty shook his head slowly. "I'll go along with you for a while, but I know I must be crazy to do it."

They pushed through to the little stream. There the tracks disappeared again. "See there, Shorty. He's not so smart. That's the oldest trick in the book."

"Yah, an old trick for a man," Shorty answered morosely. "Deer don't hide their trail in the water."

Father didn't answer this. He had to decide whether to try upstream or down. He headed up on the theory that the deer would head for the cover of the standing timber. He had guessed correctly. Just when they were beginning to wonder if they had chosen wrongly, there were the tracks showing clearly where the deer had gone up the bank.

"That's strange," Father puzzled. "He could have made it a lot harder for us here if he'd wanted to."

"He wants to keep us interested, not to make us give up and go back," countered Shorty ominously.

Now the trail led straight towards the trees, just as Father had expected. Animals don't care much for snow falling on them and will take shelter if they can. But still the deer took advantage of every little tree, every clump of brush to avoid being seen.

They reached the timber at last, and the land rose more steeply. The trail led directly uphill, and there was less chance of seeing their quarry. Still they pressed on, caught up in that obsessive excitement of the hunting animal that is part of our genetic heritage, and which those who have never felt it can never understand, although they too carry it within them.

But the chase looked hopeless now. If the deer could elude them in the open burn, there was no chance at all of seeing it here unless it chose to let them.

Father knew this, but he also knew that animals – just like humans – grow careless when they feel that they are safe, and he was determined to keep trying for a while yet.

The land levelled out into a bench, an area of flattish ground a couple of hundred yards wide. A fair-sized creek ran through it diagonally before turning abruptly to flow into the valley – fair-sized, that is, in the context of the surroundings. It was about a foot deep and three feet across, the water that deep brown colour of coast forest streamlets. The tracks led to it, but they didn't continue on the other side. The two hunters stopped, looked around.

"The wading trick won't work here," Father said, "the ground is too level. Up or down?"

"You pick," said Shorty, uneasy again.

"Up it is then."

Off they went, one on each side of the stream and about ten feet away from it. They had scarcely gone a hundred feet when they came to a rock face down which the water slid noisily. They looked up it. Almost forty feet of sheer vertical rock, green with moss, a few ferns growing in the cracks. A mountain climber would have a hard time scaling it.

"If he got over that, I'm not going to try following him," joked Father.

They scouted around for signs, found none, and headed back down, this time a bit further from the water in case they had missed something. On they went, past the place where the tracks had led, until their way was blocked by a huge fallen fir tree lying directly across the stream. It was head high, covered with a dense growth of young trees rooted in the rotting bark. These in turn were covered with a layer of unbroken snow. Branches and debris had collected in front of the tree where the swirling, partially blocked water had collected in a deep coffee-coloured pool half covered by several inches of thick yellow foam. There were no tracks anywhere, save those they had followed. Again, Father coursed the ground like a baffled hound. Back to the rock face, down again on the other side to the big log, then back up to where Shorty was standing watching him. As he came near, his friend said in a voice made hoarse with emotion:

"Hal, that's it. I'm finished. If you go on from here, you go alone. For God's sake man, wake up! Surely you don't still think that's a deer standing out there waiting for us?"

Father looked at him but made no answer. He walked over to the fallen tree, then along it to the great upturned root. He went around behind it, back to the stream. He watched the dark water welling up from under the obstruction, then started across, intending to walk right around the tree. He tried once more to imagine what he would have done. Then he saw the answer, for the tracks of the deer showed plainly in the snow a few yards downstream of him, where it had walked out of the water after swimming under the tree through that black and treacherous pool, and surfacing up on the other side. A feat so improbable that it hadn't occurred to Father that it could be done. He looked up, feeling a sudden intuition, and there was the deer, no more than a hundred feet away, standing in full view in an open space between the trees. It was side on, its head turned towards him, looking at him, its body darkly wet, its huge rack of horns shining golden against the snow.

For a long moment their eyes locked. An animal always knows when you see it and runs off as soon as your eyes focus on it. But not this one.

Then Father remembered what he was there for. He swung his gun swiftly to his shoulder, aligning the sights onto that spot by the ear that would bring instant death, as he had done so many times before.

But this time, something stayed his hand. He could feel the deer's eyes riveted on him. He thought about the chase it had led them, the calm intelligence it had shown. And then in a way it never had before, the wildness and beauty of the great animal, so at home here in the snow and trees, hit a soft spot that Father hadn't known he possessed, and he lowered the gun without firing.

"And then," he told me, "the strangest thing happened. I had a sort of vision of an open space under the trees. There wasn't any snow. Against the dark ground was a pile of bones shining white and bare. Human bones. There were skulls lying scattered about. It must have been spring. The leaves were bright green. It was just a flash, a quick glimpse, that passed as quick as an eyeblink. But when I looked up, the deer was gone."

He went back around the root. Shorty was standing near the pool.

"It dove under the log," Father said to him, "and came up on the other side. I almost got a shot at it."

"You mean it turned into a fish. Nothing else could get under that log. Look at it!" He pointed to the pool. "I'm going back now. Are you coming?"

"Shorty was scared," Father told me. "I had never seen Shorty scared before. A wounded grizzly bear wouldn't have scared Shorty. I got that end-of-the-world feeling again, and I thought of that picture of the pile of bleached bones lying under the trees. I thought of that big deer out there, waiting for us to follow him. What would he do next? I thought of what nerve it took to go into that dark pool of water carrying those horns, not knowing if you could make it through or not. I thought, 'Why did he do it?' He didn't have to. He could have made fools of us on that mountain, in those trees. He wasn't scared of us, or why would he stop and watch us? I asked myself these questions, but I had no answers.

"I said, 'Come on Shorty. It's getting late. Let's go home.'" ❖

Kalpalin – an Aboriginal Metropolis

BY HOWARD WHITE

During the 1950s and 1960s when I was growing up in the Sunshine Coast fishing village of Pender Harbour, I was never short of information on the Spanish and English explorers who had first charted local waters in the late 1700s and 1800s. Along the coast there were monuments to Captain George Vancouver, and local place names provided a daily reminder of his personal interests—his heroes (Nelson Island), his moods (Desolation Sound), his family (Sarah Point). Many place names such as Texada Island, Malaspina Strait and Favada Point also commemorated the brief visitations of the Spanish, who churned through the territory alongside their English rivals in such a panic to find the fabled Northwest Passage they failed to notice Sechelt Inlet, Pender Harbour, and a host of other major geographical features. In addition, history buffs were forever rediscovering the explorers' journals and highlighting passages where local landmarks had rated a brief mention. Writers like Roderick Haig-Brown and Hubert Evans wrote juvenile adventure novels based on Vancouver's and David Thompson's brief weeks of disappointment here, and centennial celebrations spotlighted the momentary presence of the long-ago superstars of European colonization.

What I never could find much about was the other pioneers, the ones who had been here for thousands of years before the anxious European visitors and were to remain hundreds of years after—the aboriginal inhabitants. Their presence was hard to ignore in Pender Harbour.

Not that there were many living, breathing Indians still around when I first saw Pender Harbour in 1950—the aged chief Dan Johnson and his wife lived in a tumbledown shack on a reserve in Garden Bay that was said to be laden with graves, ghosts and artifacts; Eugene and Myrtle Paul lived on a landlocked scrap of land in Gerrans Bay and the Julius family lived near the mouth of the Harbour on a barren group of islets locals referred to as the "Indian Islands," ignoring the map name of Skardon Islands. The white people had everything else, but there were abundant signs that it had been very different once upon a time. The much-indented shoreline of the one-and-

a-half-mile-long harbour was paved with bones—human bones.

My school chum Ab Haddock and I lived on opposite sides of Gerrans Bay a stone's throw from a small group of islets local legend recorded as an Indian graveyard, and he used to make me jealous with all the nifty artifacts he dug up on them, but the rest of us kids lacked the nerve to disturb them for fear of awakening smoldering embers of the last smallpox epidemic, which to us seemed to lurk still close at hand.

Indian history hovered in the air of the harbour. Clues were everywhere. At Sakinaw Bay you could still trace among the barnacled beach rocks vague outlines of the elaborate stone fish trap which pioneer ethnologist Charles Hill-Tout had described as a masterpiece of stone-age engineering a half-century earlier; shortly thereafter loggers perched an A-frame on the nearby bluff to skid logs out of Sakinaw Lake and promptly obliterated all sign of the ancient wonder. Atop Mount Daniel you could still discern outlines of the stone circles which were placed in worship of the moon by pubescent girls, according to local historian Lester Peterson, but which Hill-Tout described with equal assurance as tombs of the dead. Elders Ann Quinn and Theresa Jeffries say they were simply used by girls "to meditate and prepare themselves for marriage." The stones remain in their circles to this day.

My belief after a lifetime of excavating around Pender Harbour—not as an archaeologist, but as an interested ditch digger—is that there must have been almost continuous settlement around the entire forty miles of harbour shoreline. I once had a job installing a sewer system on the Sallahlus reserve at Canoe Pass and found myself digging down in ancient fire ash and clamshell deposits to a depth of six feet, encountering more than a few human bones along the way. There was another large deposit of bone-laden midden soil at Irvine's Landing at the mouth of the Harbour, and sizable ones at Gerrans Bay and on the fertile mudflats at the head of Oyster Bay, a site known as Smeshalin to the Sechelt (shishalh.) (For old time's sake I have used the more familiar anglicized spellings of Sechelt words but follow with the official phonetic spelling on first usage.) When my father and I were excavating basements around Pender Harbour in the 1960s I became accustomed to rooting up cooking rocks and clamshell anywhere there was a pocket of dirt big enough to sink a muckstick into. Many sites were chock-full of human remains.

I knew from reading about better-documented sites in Huronia that many generations of occupancy upon a single campsite could result in only a few inches of permanent midden soil—and in Pender Harbour there were places the midden soil was eight feet thick. What had gone on here? From my dad's old buddy Clarence Joe, a ranking member of the Tsonai (ts'unay) clan in Jervis Inlet, I learned that Pender Harbour had been a "winter village" where all the far-flung Sechelt communities congregated in the wintertime for dancing and trading. But how many people gathered there? What kind of houses did they have? What did they do when they were all gathered together? Clarence and other contemporary Sechelt were disappointingly vague on these points. When I went to the University of BC, I enrolled in anthropology, hoping I might find some more specific answers.

Alas, my studies only confirmed that information on Sechelt prehistory was extremely sketchy. None of the great ethnologists who had studied the Haida and Kwakiutl in such exhaustive detail had bothered to check in on the Sechelt, for reasons that became clear to me later. However, I did discover the reason for the numerous clamshell middens around Pender Harbour. It had once been the site of one of the largest and most important aboriginal village sites in the Pacific Northwest—an authentic aboriginal metropolis.

Only scattered fragments of this amazing history now remain, and it has taken a good many years of sleuth work to piece together even a general outline of the Sechelt and their magnificent headquarters in Pender Harbour.

Before the arrival of European explorers in the late 1700s, the Sunshine Coast had been shared since the last ice age by three different tribes of native Indians, the Squamish (Howe Sound), the Sechelt (Sechelt Peninsula), and the Sliammon (Powell River). By all accounts they were an exceptional people, each in their own way as unlike the

Early view of Porpoise Bay showing tradional Sechelt dugout.

standard run of Northwest Coast Indian as the modern Sunshine Coaster is unlike the pinstriped denizen of Vancouver's Howe Street.

All of the Sunshine Coast tribes belonged to the Coast Salish linguistic family and enjoyed a comparatively prosperous existence owing to their benign climate and an abundance of easily obtained food, principally salmon, herring, venison and berries. The Coast Salish have never enjoyed the renown accorded by white Indian-fanciers to the Haida and Kwakiutl, probably because the Salish didn't erect forests of totem poles, didn't carve sea-going war canoes, and didn't produce world-class art—except on one notable occasion. On the other hand, they didn't use the bodies of freshly killed slaves for boat bumpers. What they did do was create a social order that came closer to that of modern democracies in terms of respect for human life and individual freedom. Among the Northern tribes, only those born to noble families could hope to achieve spiritual power through membership in the cannibal and dog-eating

societies, but every member of a Salish tribe had the opportunity to seek his or her individual "sulia" or "power" through a spirit quest that was open to all comers, and leadership was based on merit as much as on inherited privilege. There was no single, all-powerful chief, but a collective of male and female leaders all honoured with the same respectful term, "si3'm" or in Sechelt, "hiwus."

In their heyday, the Sechelt occupied the bulk of the territory now comprising the Sunshine Coast with some eighty villages. So numerous were the lodge fires of the Sechelt Nation elders used to speak of a time when there was "one big smoke" from Gower Point to Saltery Bay. The main tribal groupings were centred around four principal villages at xenichen (at the head of Jervis Inlet), Tsonai (at Deserted Bay, Jervis Inlet), Tuwanek (in Sechelt Inlet) and Kalpalin (Pender Harbour.) Unlike most other Coast Salish tribes, who stayed put in their ancestral villages year round, the Sechelt congregated for the winter in one composite mega-village at

The Story of Ts'kahl
BY GILBERT JOE

The Sechelt people, in their system, had a purpose for everyone. There was the chiefs, the elders and the warriors. Some of these warriors, by today's standards they would have been called psychopaths. But the aboriginal people along the coast used to be very warlike among themselves, mainly for food.

We had a terrible-tempered man, his name was Ts'kahl (ts`uKal)—a prominent individual respected by all the Sechelt people. He actually killed a couple of Indian people just for standing in his way. But there was a place for men like him in our society, we made them warriors.

During the summer months our forefathers would pack up, dismantle their lodges, and go up the Inlet to collect and preserve their food for winter. The elder men and women stayed home to look after the community.

One summer when the warriors were gone, the Kwakiutl came down from Nimpkish and raided our village, killing all the people except one young woman of high birth, Wipple-Wit, who was taken as a slave.

When the warriors returned they found pieces of their loved ones' bodies hanging from trees and scattered along the beach. They were very angry. The chief and elders decided to retaliate, and when they wanted to retaliate they wanted to do it in good fashion. So they negotiated with the Cowichan for their greatest warrior, Tzouhalem. And they negotiated with the Squamish for their greatest warrior and his name was Luhma.

They gathered all the Sechelt warriors—the strongest and the best—to go up to Nimpkish and retaliate against the Kwakiutls. They got in their big canoes with their provisions and spears and they had Spanish muskets.

Kalpalin (kalpilin) on the shores of Pender Harbour. Although contemporary band publications place their original population at 20,000, scientific estimates range between 5,000 and 8,000. Even if the lowest estimate is correct, it would have made Kalpalin more densely populated in 1800 than Pender Harbour was in 1996 – and that was just counting local residents. During big feasts, potlatches (tl'eʔenaks) or trading days, that number would be swelled by other Salish groups visiting from upcoast, downcoast, the Fraser River, the Gulf Islands, Vancouver Island and Puget Sound.

The Sechelt have no tradition of having migrated from anywhere else; their creation myths relate that the creator sent the *spelemulh*, divine but mortal ancestors of the Sechelt people, down to each village from the sky. Other Coast Salish village sites have been dated as far back as 9,000 years but little archaeological work has been done on the Sechelt and most of the midden sites are now gouged up by logging or, like the great Sawquamain site in Garden Bay, paved over with residential subdivisions.

The Salish had an admirable grasp of what really mattered in life. They were tremendous workers and they laboured mightily all summer putting up dried salmon and making salal berry leather as well as thousands of other labour-intensive tasks involved in maintaining well-run stone-age households, like weaving watertight baskets of cedar root and washing used ones with a putrefied fungus known as "thunder shit" (xwat'Klmunach). Everyday dress consisted of aprons made of deer hide or woven from cedar bark. Cedar bark was also woven into blankets and robes, as was wool from special long-haired dogs and mountain goat. Rope and twine for fishing line and nets were woven from nettle fibre. Plentiful stands of red cedar provided easily worked building materials for dugout canoes, feast bowls and plank-walled dwellings, some of which were enormous.

Now Indian people long ago were psychically inclined. Because they had no newspapers or TVs or anything to deter them, they had very powerful minds. They had medicine men that had great psychic powers who could communicate with their minds.

So when the Sechelt warriors headed up to Nimpkish to retaliate, they went by Sliammon at night and they didn't touch their canoes with their paddles. They passed there at night so the Sliammon wouldn't know they were going by. And they did the same at Klahoose. And they did the same at Homalco. Every community between here and Nimpkish they passed without being noticed because if somebody from one of the villages had seen them passing by, they could have sent a message up to the Kwakiutls with their minds. So the warriors didn't want to take that chance.

They made it up to Nimpkish and they waited until dark when the people went to sleep. Then they went onto the beach. Ts'kahl, Tzouhalem and Luhma began their war-whoops in their fierce, enormous voices. They frightened the people of the Nimpkish village so much that they fell into a shambles, giving the warriors enough time to run up the beach and take their revenge.

On the beach, Ts'kahl saw a person rolling toward the water in a cedar blanket as if trying to get away. He went up to the person and was about to spear it when he heard a voice say, "hoy-la tsi-loy wipple-wit." (It's me—Wipple-Wit.") He stopped just in time.

So the warriors brought Wipple-Wit back home. And that was the last time there was a battle between the Kwakiutl and the Sechelt people.

According to Hill-Tout, who studied the Sechelt in the summer of 1902, Sechelt houses had "a platform about two feet high and five or six feet broad erected all around the inside walls. This served as seats or lounges for the occupants during the day, and during the night as beds. Some ten or twelve feet above this platform small isolated cubicles or sleeping rooms were constructed... Each family partitioned off its allotment from the rest by means of hanging mats." Anthropologist Homer Barnett, who visited the Sechelt in 1935, reported seeing only one house which was excavated, and that only to the depth of one step below ground level. In *The Story of the Sechelt Nation* Lester Peterson reports that "Sechelt lodges were filled with dried meats, smoked fish, dried berries and fruits. Chests, *wihk'-ahm*, were filled with regalia – masks, cloaks, drums, rattles, and other paraphernalia needed at ceremonies." Hill-Tout contradicts this, saying "they did not store their winter supplies in the dwellings, but cached them in the woods. Only a few days' supply was ever carried home. This peculiar custom was due to the marauding proclivities of the neighbouring Yacultas, who made periodic forays upon their settlement and carried off all they could lay their hands upon. It was unsafe,

therefore, to keep a large store of food by them." Hill-Tout's informant, Charlie Roberts, was born four decades before Peterson's main informant, Basil Joe, and the inconsistency between generations may reflect fading memories of inter-tribal hostilities during later historic times, but there is no shortage of evidence to indicate that in their heyday the peaceful Sechelt were a favourite target for raiding by leaner and meaner tribes to the north.

The work of the Salish summer was performed with the singular aim of freeing the winter for social activities. Anthropologists are fond of referring to the winter activities of the Salish as "ceremonials" which they manage to depict as some kind of joyless paleolithic ritual. My old Squamish friend Dominic Charlie, who kept performing his sensational leaping deer dance until he was in his eighties, remembered it differently. "In them old times," Dominic told me, "we just dance and dance all winter long. Just dance and dance. Everybody he go to that big house and dance all night long and all day. All winter keep doing that. Oh, we had great times in them old times."

Great times. That's what the Salish winter was really all about. Most people had their own special dance which had come to them in a dream or vision

Sechelt men show off a morning's catch at the white village west of the reserve. Despite closeness, the two villages remain separate worlds. Photo: BCARS D-07509.

accompanied by a song, and often gave them a special power associated with an animal. One renowned hunter imitated killer whales in his dance. He had got this dance when he once approached a beach where people were dancing around a campfire, but turned into killer whales and swam away when he approached. In the dream that followed he got not only the dance and a song, but the killer whale's power to hunt seals, sea-lions and porpoises. Another prominent man had the wolf dance. He got it when he fell and wounded his leg while stripping bark from a tree. When he awoke a wolf was licking his wound. In his dream he received a song featuring the cry of the wolf and a dance in which he ate the flesh of live dogs. Men's dances tended to be associated with major animals like the bear and mountain goat, while women were often left with lesser spirits like the duck, crane, quail, and even the blowfly.

Dances by ordinary Sechelt people didn't go in for the special effects some of the northern tribes used to imitate their animal allies, and generally eschewed masks and costumes in favour of convential gestures (leaping for a deer, flapping arms for a bird). Face paint was used, but costumes tended to be the usual buckskins worn every day.

Winter ceremonials also included events of a more distinctly spiritual nature, initiation rites for youngsters taking possession of their own special dances, and performances by medicine men. Sechelt shamans were particularly noted for their miraculous performances. One involved the handling of red-hot coals and rocks, and the eating of fire. Another featured the dancer making a dramatic bloody slash along the length of his thigh, while another shot blood from his mouth. The ts`unay elder Joe La Dally told anthropologist Homer Barnett of an occasion when an eminent shaman named Kaltopa was called to attend a dying man. He brought with him the skins of seven different animals – otter, mink, raccoon, fox, loon, eagle and marten. After singing his spirit song, he blew on each skin and it came to life, scampering around on the floor uttering its natural cry. He then covered his head with a blanket and began to grope on the floor in search of the patient's missing soul. His

own spirit was thought to have departed from his body at this point because at length he uttered a "whoo-ing" noise as if returning from a great distance. Finally the shaman rose, holding the retrieved soul in his hands. When it was returned to its rightful place the patient showed immediate signs of recovery, and his brother asked the shaman if he knew who'd taken the errant soul. The shaman said that he indeed did, whereupon the brother requested the evil-doer be put to death. The shaman again covered his head and began groping on the floor. After about half an hour the sounds of the returning spirit were heard once more, and the shaman lept to his feet to reveal in the palm of his hand a tiny human body. He held the miniature form over the fire and squeezed it till blood ran out between his fingers, then dropped the small shape into the flames. At that moment, according to legend, a well-known Comox shaman keeled over stone dead.

His duties completed, Kaltopa deflated his skins, packed up, and left. The purpose of the skins had been to watch over the patient while the medicine man was out of his body stalking his foe in the spirit realm. Barnett was able to obtain a corroborating version of this story from another Sechelt elder, Charlie Roberts, who added that Kaltopa's return was assisted by other Sechelt shamans who guided him back with choruses of their own "whoo-ing" in answer to his. Roberts said that he'd seen another shaman who could perform the miracle of bringing animal skins to life, and in addition possessed a big quartz crystal he could activate to dance and whirl around on the floor with a whining sound. Shamanic performances of this kind were a regular and popular feature of winter dances, along with feasting and potlatching, the ceremonial giving of property to enhance status. There were also lively trading extravaganzas, especially among the Sechelt, who have always been great wheeler-dealers.

Kalpalin's principal settlement at Sawquamain, on the north shore of Garden Bay, was crowded with seven huge longhouses, four ranked one behind the other while the other three ran crosswise further inland. Some had shed-type single-slope roofs and others the peaked variety. Each had an attached woodshed and a spacious outdoor platform suitable for the staging of potlatches, an architectural feature Sechelt elder Gilbert Joe has referred to as "the Sunshine Coast's first sun-decks." Like modern-day leisure homes which announce themselves to passing traffic as "Taki-Teasy" or "Dunworkin" (my favourite is "Sechelter"), each of the Sawquamain lodges had its own nickname. Lodge number one was called "Right On the Beach" and lodge number two, "Back Side House." It had no exterior decoration, but inside, the support posts were carved into seals, sea lions and killer whales. The third house, "Down In the Hole," had a thunderbird painted on the front. Lodge number four had a single-slope shed roof and was the largest building on the site. Lodge six had a painted welcome figure straddling the doorway and seven had a thunderbird painted across the front. There were no totem poles but "Right On the Beach" had a sea lion head carved onto the end of the ridgepole and lodge five had posts topped with carvings of eagles. The largest house Peterson records as the Kluh-uhn'-ahk-ahwt (tl'epotlatchAenaKawt or "potlatch house"), which he describes as a kind of Sechelt Parthenon, used only when the far-flung affiliate villages were gathered together for communal events. Salish houses weren't as finely crafted as those of the northern tribes, but they were bigger. The explorer Simon Fraser observed one near Chilliwack which was 800 feet long and 300 feet wide, and Charlie Roberts told Hill-Tout the greatest of the lodges at Sawquamain towered fifty feet in height.

The Sechelt were highly vulnerable to attack by other Indian tribes, a vulnerability increased by their relative wealth and their nonviolent nature. The word "fort" occurs frequently in Sechelt place names, and according to Peterson a real fort replete with wooden pallisade and moat stood until historic times near the head of Jervis Inlet. Another fort existed on Thormanby Island, where the exposed Squawklot (sxwelap) village made frequent use of it to fend off seagoing marauders from Kwakiutl territory. My old school chum Ron Remmem, whose family home in Pender Harbour was close to the Sechelt's long-vanished winter capital of Sawquamain, used to talk about finding what looked like an ancient fort site on the slopes of nearby Mount Daniel. This matches stories Peterson collected of a fort on Mount Daniel which was used to shelter women and children during raids on Sawquamain. Barnett reports the big houses of Sawquamain had "subterranean retreats ready for use in case of surprise attacks...entered by tunnels leading from hidden openings inside." Basil Joe's son Clarence used to tell me his people also kept sentries posted on Mount Daniel – and at many other places including Cape Cockburn to the north and Spyglass Hill to the south – to provide early warning of any suspicious traffic in surrounding waters. All of which adds up to a fairly pervasive sense of vulnerability.

Most raids were two-bit affairs perpetrated by piratical rovers who picked off small groups of women and elders left unprotected during fishing or hunting forays, but large-scale massacres were not unknown. Peterson mentions a grassy flat east of Cockburn Bay on Nelson Island which got its name, Swalth (skwelh,) "from the fact that much blood was spilt there." He also used to tell me that the rocky knoll next to the property I grew up on at Madeira Park "was forever cursed by a powerful medicine man because of the slaughter suffered there by his people at the hands of early nineteenth century raiders."

The destruction of this once great Native nation began early on. The Roman Catholic missionary Father Leon Fouquet of the Oblate Order visited Kalpalin in 1860, urging all to abandon the beliefs of their ancestors and accept the God of the white man. Not surprisingly, Fouquet was sent packing. But only three years later, the Sechelt invited the Oblates back and willingly submitted themselves to Christian teaching by Father Paul Durieu. By 1871 he had administered the sacrament of confirmation to the entire Sechelt tribe, a record worthy of envy even by his contemporary William Duncan, the Anglican missionary who created a similar "Indian city in the wilderness" among the Tsimshian at Metlakatla. Some writers interpret the Sechelt's remarkable turnabout simply as a case

Sechelt Indian band. After banning traditional winter festivities, priests tried to fill the gap by teaching their converts church-approved pastimes. Photo: BCARS F-02405.

of children of darkness seeing the light, but there is a less glamorous explanation. In 1862 the worst smallpox epidemic in west coast history swept like a tsunami through the coast's Indian population, devastating the Sechelt. It was in an attitude of defeat and despair that they turned back to the missionaries, but they may have had a more pointed reason yet. The Sechelt embraced the belief, universal throughout aboriginal cultures, that the world of the spirit ruled directly and absolutely over the world of matter, and the most persuasive evidence of superior force in the world of spirit was the ability to cause illness in chosen victims. When the white man appeared accompanied by a plague of new illnesses far more devastating than anything conjured up by the most powerful Indian medicine man, wiping out whole Indian nations while leaving whites untouched, Native peoples could not help but view it as evidence of some dread new spiritual super-power on the white man's side. When the

missionaries stepped forward claiming to speak for the Great Spirit of the white man and specifically threatening more illness if the Indians failed to adopt Christianity, native peoples fell on their knees in droves, but not, one would assume, for the love of Jesus. As the plagues continued they must have felt like victims of biological warfare, ready to do or say anything that would spare their families from the wrathful God of the white man.

Duncan made his greatest breakthrough by warning a general assembly of Tsimshian unbelievers they were about to taste God's wrath just as the 1862 smallpox epidemic was sweeping down upon them, and the Oblates apparently seized upon similar tactics. As anthropologist Edwin M. Lemert noted in *The Life and Death of an Indian State*, "sermons delivered by the (Oblate) priests...bore directly on persons and events...Thus epidemics of disease became grim evidence of wrongdoing by the Indians." When the Oblates told the Sechelt in the

Over 2,000 people showed up for dedication of new Our Lady of the Rosary church on June 10, 1890. Threat of flogging assured good attendance at church events.

aftermath of the 1862 holocaust the only way to save themselves was by adopting Christian teaching, it is an understatement to say they probably took it literally.

In 1868 Durieu founded a central mission at an unoccupied site the Sechelt frequented only seasonally because it was so exposed to weather and to attack by marauding Yacultas, it lacked fresh drinking water and generally didn't have much to recommend it from an Indian point of view. This was Chatelech, the site of the modern-day village of Sechelt. Over the next three decades the Oblates forged a Christian community at Sechelt which became the showpiece of "The Durieu System," a theocratic regime featuring police-state discipline, afterward replicated at Oblate missions among the Sliammon, Klahoose, Homalco, Lillooet and others. Durieu was a strict puritan who didn't allow his own priests to drink wine in private – true privation to a Frenchman – and in one favourite anecdote broke up Sechelt preparations for a soccer tournament with the Nanaimos, confiscated the ball and ordered players and spectators alike to get to work ditching a swamp. Durieu espoused the belief that "Indians are only big children..." and governed accordingly. The whole village was compelled to rise each morning at the first bell and attend church for prayers. An evening bell called them for a second daily round of prayers each evening. Shortly following, a curfew bell was the signal for all lights to be put out. The punishment for missing church was the same as for adultery: forty lashes. On one occasion the flogging got so far out of hand one of Durieu's lieutenants was convicted and jailed by civil court.

Native culture was rigorously suppressed. As Bishop E.M. Bunoz wrote in a warm appreciation of his predecessor's system in 1941, "Our Indians had to give up all of their old fashioned amusements because they contained some traces of paganism and superstition. So they made bonfires with their century-old totem poles. They had to burn rattles, expensive coats and other paraphernalia of the medicine men...'Potlatches' great and small were forbidden. Gambling, dancing and some winter festivities had to be abandoned. Bishop Durieu strictly exacted the abolition of the above practices because they were apposed to pure Christianity, but he knew well that the Indians had to have some amusements and that the pagan feasts had to replaced by Christian ones."

Under Durieu's control the Sechelt made a name for themselves by building a European-style townsite similar to Metlakatla, by touring a brass band and theatre troupe that staged elaborate passion plays around BC, and by diligently applying themselves to such non-traditional economic pursuits as logging, commercial fishing and commercial hunting for the fresh meat trade in Vancouver. Viewing the results of Durieu's cultural makeover of the Sechelt three decades after it began, ethnologist Hill-Tout reported "Of all the native races of this province, they are probably the most modified by white influences. They are now, outwardly at least, a civilized people, and their lives compare favourably with the better class of peasants of Western Europe. Their permanent tribal home, or headquarters, contains about a hundred well-built cottages, many of them two-storied, and some of them having as many as six rooms. Each house has its own garden plot attached to it in which are grown European fruits and vegetables. In the centre of the whole stands an imposing church, which cost the tribe nearly $8,000 a few years ago. Nearby, they have a commodious and well-built meeting room, or public hall, capable of holding 500 persons or more, and a handsome pavilion or band-stand fronts the bay. They possess also a convenient and effective waterworks system of their own...every street has its hydrants at intervals of forty or fifty yards.

"As a body, the Sechelt are, without doubt, the most industrious and prosperous of all the native peoples of this province...they owe their tribal and individual prosperity mainly, if not entirely, to the Fathers of the Oblate Mission."

In fact the Sechelt had not flourished in the charge of the church, but had continued to vanish at an alarming rate until by the time of the first official census in 1881, there were only 167 survivors left from the original population of five thousand or more. The prim little community Hill-Tout viewed so approvingly in 1902 was but a sad remnant of the sprawling aboriginal nation that had united all the inlets and islands of the Sunshine Coast in "one smoke" a hundred years earlier. In the hundred years since, the Sechelt have recovered only slowly. By 1993 official band membership numbered 444 residents, with another 400 living off reserve.

Most of the fabulous repertoire of songs, dances and ceremonial art which had enlivened the great festival season at Kalpalin was lost, but some were transferred to neighboring tribes on Vancouver Island who still perform with them today.

One outstanding artifact remaining from prehistoric times is the "Sechelt Image," a 20-inch tall granite statuette discovered under a tree root by boys playing at Selma Park in 1921. I am informed that Sechelt elders of today view the figure as a mother holding her child *only* – with the emphasis on "only" because other observers, like anthropologist Wilson Duff, describe it as "the very image of masculine strength, stated in the metaphor of sex. His head is powerfully masculine, and he clasps a huge phallus; the whole boulder, seen backwards and upside down, is phallic in form."

I went down to Sechelt just before writing this to check it over once more, and I'm afraid I have to side with Duff. For me, any doubt about the sexual connotation of the work is resolved by taking the rear view, where the whole sculpture appears as a massive phallus replete with bulging veins reminiscent of a work by contemporary Sunshine Coast painter Maurice Spira. But the sculptor of the stone image goes even further, equipping the front of his piece with a prominent vulva as well.

Was some antique wit trying to sum up the entire sexual experience of humankind at one go? Or is it just something in the water Sunshine Coast artists drink? Whatever the answer, Duff pronounced the Sechelt Image "a great work of stone sculpture" and it inspired the Director of the Victoria Art Gallery, Richard Simmins, to make it the centrepiece of "Images: Stone: B.C.", a seminal exhibition of Northwest Coast Indian stone sculpture which toured Canada in 1975. A replica of this enigmatic, powerful masterwork, along with some good examples of Sechelt weaving and carving, can be viewed in the band's Tems Swiya Museum in Sechelt.

Today's Sechelt have maintained their head start in terms of mastering mainstream economic and political life. They have been involved in the operation of an offshore trawler, a local airline, a salmon hatchery, an office and cultural complex, a large gravel-mining project, a McDonalds restaurant franchise and other business enterprises. But it is in the political arena that the Sechelt have most distinguished themselves. From the earliest times when Chief Tom of the ts'unay made land claims representations to Victoria, through the activism of such leaders as Chief Julius, Joe La Dally, Dan Paull, Reg Paull, Stan Dixon and Clarence Joe – a consummate statesman who on different occasions addressed both the Canadian House of Commons and the United Nations – the Sechelt charted their own course through Canadian politics, far in advance of most other First Nations groups. Their first goal was to free themselves from the shackles of the Canadian Indian Act, which deprived them of the full rights of citizenship and greatly encumbered the free exercise of their renowned mercantile abilities, which sometimes outshine their modern-day neighbours on the old Chatelech site. Their long campaign finally culminated in the successful passage of Bill C-93, The Sechelt Indian Band Self-Government Act of 1986, making them the first band in Canada to achieve native self-government.

This in itself proved controversial within the community of First Nations, since the Sechelt had taken a very pragmatic view of self government, one characterized by the Grand Council of Crees as "identical to the model of the municipalities." This is not quite true since the Sechelt are given extra-municipal powers over education, social services, health, and public order, and section 38 of the *Self Government Act* declares that the "constitution of the Band or the law of the Band" can take precedence over the laws of British Columbia. Other bands held out for something closer to full provincial status and denounced the Sechelt solution as a sellout. The Sechelt view the grander claims as impracticable, and hold that freedom to conduct their own affairs as full Canadian citizens free from the strictures of the Indian Act is no small gain. Since 1986 more bands across Canada, whose own campaigns for self-government remain stalled, have been taking a second look at the Sechelt model, and the Nishga settlement of 1996 owes much to it, but for the most part the Sechelt remain defiantly out of step with their brethren on the national stage.

At the same time the Sechelt feel sadly cut off from the traditions of their aboriginal past, and they carry on few ceremonial activities compared to the neighboring Cowichan and Squamish. They pursue a vigorous language preservation project with the help of Dr. Ronald Beaumont of the University of B.C. and several families have revived the practice of giving potlatches (tl'e?enaks) to bestow traditional names, which they research in old church records. Elder Mary Craigan had tears in her eyes as she recounted to me her experience attending a Cowichan ceremony where she witnessed some of the ancient songs and dances which were once performed by her ancestors at Kalpalin. It was the first time she had heard them but they had worked a powerful spell over her she had no words to describe, as if pulling at something deep inside. A traditional medicine man from outside has begun visiting the band, 130 years after shamanistic practices were banned by the Oblates, and Craigan struggles alongside other elders to excavate memories of their people's past to fulfill younger members' reawakening thirst for tribal identity, but it is hard digging. Indian or non-, who can say what their ancestors did and thought over a century ago when there has been no continuing connection and the only written record has been kept by people dedicated to breaking the connection?

Despite that century of cataclysmic upheaval, remorseless cultural domination, near-complete depopulation, and advanced dilution by foreign blood, a very powerful feeling still endures at the village core that the Sechelt are a unique people distinctly apart from the world around them. Despite Professor Hill-Tout's gleeful declaration that Bishop Durieu's master plan had succeeded in acculturating the Sechelt into "a better form of European peasant" at the beginning of this century, to step across the boundary from Municipality of Sechelt onto the Band Lands today is to enter into a special world little suspected by outsiders. How much of this is due to lingering influences of the aboriginal past which managed to seep around the proscriptions of the priests and how much is the stamp of six generations of intense economic and geo-graphical ghettoization, is hard to say. Certainly any closely related family group shaped by the pressures that have crushed down upon the Sechelt over the past 200 years could be expected to emerge with a lot of distinctive characteristics, no matter what their previous cultural history.

Meanwhile, there is no longer one single member of the Sechelt band living on the site of the once mighty Sechelt capital of Kalpalin, and viewing the modest, all-white village of 2,500 reposing on the shores of the landlocked Pender Harbour basin today, it is difficult to picture the same scene rocking under the sway of five or ten thousand buckskinned festival-goers, but if you'd dropped in between October and March a few brief centuries ago, that may well be what you'd have seen. ❖

For their many excellent suggestions in reviewing the foregoing, my special thanks go to Sechelt elders Anne Quinn and Theresa Jeffries and their niece Candy Clark. Excerpted from The Sunshine Coast, *Harbour Publishing, 1996.*

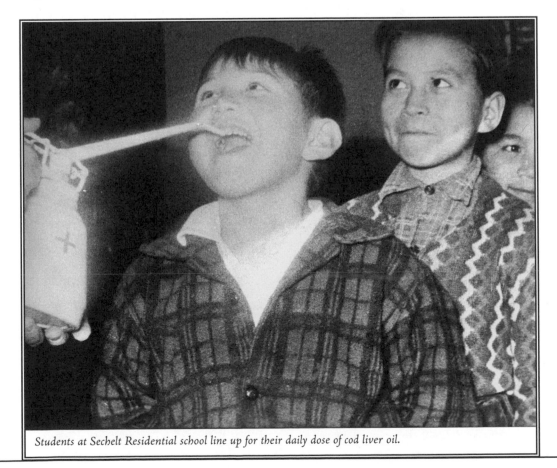

Students at Sechelt Residential school line up for their daily dose of cod liver oil.

Illustrations by Lee Croy

Please Do Not Touch the Gardenias

BY JACK SPRINGS

"*Please do not touch the gardenias. Their flowers will turn brown and fall off.*" The message was written in black marker on an index card affixed to a plastic stake that plunged into the potting soil of a small green gardenia bush. Its flowers are said to be the blooms of unrequited love and a source of symbolic comfort to morose lovers.

I had been thinking, just moments before, about something that happened years ago, when I took a summer job as a tenderman on a fish boat. I was looking forward to it, for I understood tendermen had more time to explore the coast. They were the in-between men who transported the fish from the grounds to the plant, and when not otherwise engaged, they were on their own. I would have more time to smell the flowers.

I would be the engineer! Well, to be accurate, I was engineer in name only, for the skipper, an

Australian expatriate, knew the inner workings of all things mechanical. Rolf used me more for discourse than maintenance. An overachiever in the engine room, he was possessed of the industriousness of four men and could probably have run the boat himself if he had figured out how to be in all places at once.

I wanted to make a good impression, so I showed up half an hour ahead of schedule the morning the boat was to leave. Rolf was there ahead of me. Together we fixed something green and cylindrical in the engine room, and later we moved on to the refrigeration system where I learned everything I needed to know about refrigeration systems. (It was my job to keep the fish cool.) When we finally crawled out of the room of pipes and wires I met one of the regular crew members – a "girthy" fellow by the name of Pook.

Pook was of Hawaiian ancestry and did everything he could to be mistaken for a Native Indian. "Pook?" he would say wearily, as if it were the thousandth time he had answered the question. "It's a Coast Salish word that means something like asshole." (Coast Salish was the language his Hawaiian grandmother spoke flawlessly, or so he said.) Pook would wave to every red man aboard a passing boat regardless of whether he knew them or not. The black shirt that never came off his back bore a print of a Haida-style eagle, which only heightened the illusion.

Pook was a hefty fellow, and as lazy as Rolf was industrious, an arrangement that suited him wonderfully. Because Rolf sometimes wanted to tie up the boat as well as docking it, he would often run out on deck and throw the nearest tie-up line. Pook, who also loved to be mistaken for the skipper of our boat, would stay in the wheelhouse and look out the door with his arm braced against the frame, his brow furrowed with authority as he watched the proceedings.

Yet I liked the man. And he liked me, I think, probably because I knew he was more intelligent than his dumbfounded expression would suggest – mouth agape with bottom lip protruding like an overinflated inner tube, which was the natural shape of his face at rest.

Rolf asked Pook if the new cook was here yet, to which Pook replied that he wouldn't know the cook if he saw him. I was working on deck when a woman in her early thirties came down to the boat and asked if she should drive the car down to the dock in order to unload the groceries. Now, a woman doesn't have to be especially pretty to get a lot of attention down by a fish wharf, but this one was pleasant to look at and a lot of eyes followed her back to her car. I thought this must be the delivery girl or the wife of our cook but I never dreamed for a second that she would be spending the summer aboard our boat until she stepped down off the float onto our deck and walked into the galley as if it were her own. Then the realization sank in: there was going to be a woman on board, working with us, cooking for us, eating with us, and sleeping with us. My first experience with a real live female shipmate.

What kind of a woman signs aboard a fish boat with three strange men, I wondered? She must be a woman with unarticulated fantasies about boats and rough men. A fish boat is not the regular domain of women, with the possible exception of those in glossy magazines and calendars. Those of us with vivid imaginations found it easy to suspect women who ventured into our vulgar vessels of subscribing to a non-standard code of sexual morality. Surely our new cook must understand this. We left almost the instant the groceries had been stowed in the fridge and in the ice hole below.

She had a real name but was dubbed "Cookie" almost immediately by our faux Indian deckhand. The name fit and stuck, and I shortly discovered that she was not the tart I had hoped she'd be. For one thing, she had a slight overbite with the two protruding incisors slightly separated by a gap. Not that this gap was ugly to look at. Not by any means. It lent her a girl-next-door-ish form of sweetness that was accompanied by a barely detectable lisp, as if she were perpetually sucking a peppermint candy.

Everything else about her was average in the best possible sense of the word. Her picture could have been the etching sent up in the Voyageur spacecraft, to show aliens what terrestrial females are all about. Her hair was brown and curly and hung down to her shoulders. Average height, medium build, breasts not spectacularly large or small, just right in the middle. I was in my early twenties with my hormones at high tide, so I noticed that she looked healthy, not flabby or muscular, and her bum was perfectly formed.

It didn't take long to get to know Cookie, for she was open and expressive. She liked music and played drums in a band. She was born and raised on the West Coast and she had a love of the ocean. I too had a love of the ocean and although I played no instrument I also loved music. All this I told her, but I soon found out someone else had captured her interest.

Two weeks earlier she had fallen madly in love with a gillnetter who, by happy accident, jammed with her band. She was deliriously happy when she found out our first port of call was Prince Rupert, or 'Rubert as some locals pronounce it. Her beloved would be in 'Rubert (oh joy!) along with the rest of the northern gill-net fleet. And since the first opening was delayed, they would probably be in port the day we arrived. She beamed as I told her. Thousands of plans to delight him flashed in her eyes.

I was blessed with a good grasp of the plausible, so I realized then it was futile to pursue this average-looking woman as my shipboard concubine. Instead, I offered myself as a friend.

But I was left ignorant as to the peace she made with Rolf. In an accent still thick after twenty years in this country, he confided to me his ulterior motive in hiring her. He had heard that occasionally a woman developed a fixation on her boss, doctor, or any other figure of authority. With any luck, it would happen to Cookie. Yet Rolf expressed no intention of actively encouraging her. He was, after all, a married man who would probably be more content with possibilities than realities.

By the time we reached 'Rubert, the entire crew knew about Cookie's beau. Rolf and I had accepted and even teased her about it, but Pook responded by tormenting her. He made fun of the little she knew of navigation and ship stuff. He insulted her cooking and when she got angry he said, "She's PMS-ing." That she didn't bleed to death before the end of the summer must have been a source of wonder to him.

Cookie asked for no special privileges and she slept in the fo'c's'le with the rest of the crew. In her only amendment to the usual sleeping practices of us males, she pinned together the curtains of her bunk while she dressed, undressed and slept. Even when she listened to her walkman the curtains were securely pinned, as much for her own privacy as our comfort. And the only liberty we had to give up was the casual leak over the side of the boat. Yet Pook often complained about the loss of this particular privilege and lashed out in a way that was pure Pook. In fact, I think that was the only time Cookie completely lost control. One morning there was a shriek that blasted through the toilet walls followed

by a blood oath to kill the next man to pee on the toilet seat.

And all in all, I think Cookie enjoyed the summer. We travelled north to the community of Port Simpson, or 'Shimshin as it was pronounced locally. There we stayed for a few days and went for walks. Namu was another town we visited, and we hiked along the boardwalk to the lake and then strolled along the white pearly beach. Occasionally we explored the grand old buildings that had been built for a different kind of place than the ghost town Namu had become. These destinations were chosen by Rolf and were suspiciously more appropriate for their beauty than their convenience. Our skipper had revealed himself as a shameless romantic.

Cookie was an eager learner and showed a keen interest in nearly everything. This was her second season on the water, her first being a stint as cook on another fish boat the previous year. In the off-season she had taken a net mending course to better qualify herself as a fisherman. And at night, during the wheel watches we shared, I showed her everything I knew about navigation techniques and equipment. She was a good talker and we filled many lonely hours between daylight with engaging exchanges. There were many more wheel watches I spent alone, remembering how she looked in the green glow of the radar. Very pleasant – the radar emits a carouseling dim light that rivals candles for aesthetic effect. And paired with the hum of the engine, which can gently diffuse the sound of soft speaking voices, a wheelhouse can be an evocative location.

On our way north we passed Butedale. Cookie asked about the lights, and the three men in the wheelhouse that moment poured out the little information we had about Butedale, a small autumnal community that had seen more joyous days. Something about that location touched her in a peculiar way. Nothing out of the ordinary about the place. Lights that looked like the lights of any community, only fewer of them. No interesting features hiding in the landscape. To me the tiny village was completely unremarkable, even under the stars and in the moonlight. However, Cookie asked to be woken every time we were to pass by. This detail has stuck with me for a long time. I found it remarkable that a woman could be so captured by something so completely unremarkable.

She was still impressed by eagles which would swoop to the surface of the water and pluck up cod with expanded swim bladders. When these mega birds would falter and almost head-plant themselves on the surface for overestimating the size of their quarry, she would squeal at the drama. That year was also one of the first of the El Niño currents, which brought exotic finned species up from the tropics. On the fishing grounds one of the nets had disturbed the course of a gigantic sunfish. We men found it swimming alongside our boat propelled by its stubby pectoral fins, a dorky tourist. Our first instinct was to show it, like a jewel, to our cook, as if our own perspectives had become secondary and the true measure of beauty was now more accurately judged by her.

And all the time she professed her growing love for the gillnetter. In 'Rubert they had gone out and had several wonderful times on the town. During one of these dates he officialized things, told her he loved her too. On a slow day we would be outside painting the boat and she would be singing to herself in the galley. She went on and on about what he said and what he did, saying no one has ever said that or done that before. The man could sing, dance, sweet talk and apparently walk on water. I tried my best to foster a grudge against him, but then she brought him by the boat to meet us. The beau was bigger than I had thought, but not nearly as handsome. He turned out to be a very likable guy and, try as I might, I found it difficult not to like him.

So I grew a beard. Not a great beard, for my chromosomes were conspiring against me, producing patches of blond, brown and red hair in a pattern that wouldn't allow the moustache part to join with the rest of the beard. Perhaps I thought it would make me look older, for her, but I had really given up hope. That is the reason for most of my beards – a white flag to the world. It also gave me something else to do besides fantasizing about Cookie. At every opportunity I would look in every reflective surface available – the compass window, the radar screen, the galley window. In some the beard would look fuller than others. But in the mirror I trusted most, in the toilet, it was still the sparse beard of a young man.

When the summer ended I had put on some weight and filled out my shoulders. I had dispatched the beard a week before and was now dealing with a strange facial tan. We had made our last delivery to the fish plant in Vancouver, and although the boat would head out once more, I had to stay ashore and begin my semester at university. It was time to say goodbye to the crew. I shook hands with Rolf and Pook, I would miss them, but when it came to Cookie I stretched out my arms and gave her a hearty embrace.

You know a hug is over when there is that last final squeeze. But in this hug, when I decided to step away at an appropriate interval, I felt a sharp pain in my breastbone. It shot through my entire body and caused the flesh on my back to tingle. At first I thought it must be an amulet or a pin of Cookie's that had pierced my chest, but as I recoiled from the pain a bee flew out from between us.

It wasn't until eight years later that the gardenia metaphor occurred to me. But time has shrunk till it's touched at a few points. The last I heard, Cookie is living a happy life on Lasqueti Island, in a house she shares with her gillnetter. As for me, I try not to think of gardenias, much less touch them. ❖

THE PEOPLE'S HOME MEDICAL BOOK

**BOOK I
OF THE
PEOPLE'S
HOME
LIBRARY**

BY

T. J. RITTER M.D.

GRADUATE OF BOTH THE ALLOPATHIC
AND HOMEOPATHIC SCHOOLS.
FORMERLY ASS'T. TO THE CHAIR OF THE
THEORY AND PRACTICE OF MEDICINE,
MICHIGAN STATE UNIVERSITY,
ANN ARBOR, MICH.

Published by

THE R. C. BARNUM CO.
Cleveland, Ohio—Minneapolis, Minn.
Boston, Mass.

IMPERIAL PUBLISHING CO.
TORONTO, CANADA

1919

The Doctor Book

BY MARGARET MCKIRDY

Mama allotted *The People's Home Medical Book* a position in our home alongside the Bible and the Eaton's catalogue. Its influence was greater than either. This book, edited by T.J. Ritter, M.D., formerly Assistant to the Chair of the Theory and Practice of Medicine, Michigan State University, Ann Arbor, Michigan, was published in 1919. We called it the Doctor Book.

Mama was a beautiful woman. When she was ninety, her wrinkles had a softness about them; her pink complexion and silky white curls glowed with health. The very blueness of her eyes lent sincerity to whatever she said, and there was a calmness in her mien as if she had come to terms with life. She had only one imperfection: the nail on her ring finger was slightly misshapen, and all her life there was a hairline scar along the fingertip. Mama explained the scar to anyone who admired her heavy gold ring. "That scar was there when your dad first placed the ring on my finger," she told me, explaining that Dad had chosen her even with her flaw. Actually I was seven years old, and Mama had been married a dozen years, when she got the felon.

A felon, like smallpox, is a disease of the past. I look it up in the Doctor Book.

Felon – Run-Around – Whitlow: It is generally seated immediately around and beneath the finger nail, commencing either at the side, the back, or the end of the finger. The deeper structures are affected and the pain is terrible. The tough covering of the bone is affected and pus appears next to the bone and underneath this tough covering… There is but one thing to do for this kind of felon and that is to open it early and thoroughly.

Trying to remember how Dad and Mama treated it, I read further:

Have a curved knife with both edges sharp and it should be placed in boiling water for at least 5 minutes before using. Place the patient's hand on the table with the felon side up and this is usually the palm. Put the patient's arm away from the body and stand behind the elbow. Put the knife carefully on the finger a little ways from the felon and on the side nearest the hand. Call the patient's attention to something at the other side of the room and while he is looking away press down hard with the knife and as you press down he will jerk and thus make the cut long enough. As the table is solid he cannot jerk down away from the knife and the cut will go through the covering of the bone as desired and in 10 minutes there will be very little pain.

I can't imagine anyone hoodwinking Mama into accepting this treatment. She would have read the instructions. Neither can I picture Dad being so foolish as to try. Mama did not have a forgiving nature, especially where Dad was concerned.

I look at the scar on the dining room table and remember one night when we waited dinner for Dad, who was out drinking with the boys. On his return, when he carved the chicken his unsteady hand slipped and the knife struck the table. After that, whenever Dad suggested he might be late, Mama rubbed stain into the table's wound.

No! Even when his hand was steady, she wouldn't have let him gouge her finger. So what happened? I read on:

The pus is between this covering and the bone and you must make an opening for it. If you do not, it will, after many days and nights of suffering, burrow through, and destroy much flesh.

Well, her fingernail was destroyed, and the new one was a constant reminder. But what choices did they have?

To prevent a felon apply the white of an egg with 1/2 teaspoonful of salt added. If applied in time no one need have a felon.

Mama had been remiss. With slight precaution, she could have avoided the felon. Did she think of that while she suffered the treatment? Probably, since she never attached blame in the recounting.

Soak the finger or affected part for half an hour in strong lye, or ashes and water, as hot as can be borne. Do this 2 or 3 times a day and apply a poultice of soft soap and turpentine. If the felon comes to head, lance it, poultice with lye and elm bark, and heal with some good salve.

Did Dad lance the thing before it came to a head? I think not. Mama would have attached blame.

No. As I found out eventually, my parents had taken the trip to the doctor. But the felon was slow to heal, and Mama carried the scar, attesting to imperfection, for the rest of her life.

In good Christian homes when Mama was young and well into childhood, the misfortunes we suffered were thought to be our own fault. In God's good grace, the natural state was to be alive and well. If your condition was any other, if you were unfortunate, sick, or dying, you were guilty. There were questions you must answer. How had you been remiss? What rule had you broken? What taboo had you flouted?

Of course there were skeptics even then, and people who felt their systems were too delicate to withstand harsh treatment. For these people, syrups and tonics well laced with alcohol, laudanum or morphine were available, and they were used with sometimes tragic results. But few people in rural communities took the easy way out, and when they did, they were accepting of blame.

Dad was among the skeptics. During a brief period of prohibition in our northern area, Dad could walk twenty miles to find a doctor who would prescribe rum for his cold. He strode out into the biting wind with his collar open, his head

bare. He only covered up when there was no one to witness, and when he entered the doctor's office. Perhaps the bad boy image he maintained lent adrenalin for the walk.

Women were not allowed to enjoy the reputation of being bad. One of our neighbours, whose nerve tonic imparted the whiff of alcohol to her breath, always needed a second and third sip before she informed us that she was "not strong." Her tall body shrunk into her disgrace.

Everyone in the community suffered guilt, Catholics and Calvinistic Protestants alike. The difference was that the Catholic could be absolved by the priest; the Protestant carried guilt to the grave.

When I was six, two of our young friends offered to teach my sister and me about sex. One of the boys was a Catholic, and the next time I went to play with him, he said, "I can't play with you. Father O'Connor says you're bad."

"Well then, you're bad, too."

"No I'm not. I did penance."

I wonder how much of the guilt we suffered was reinforced by the Doctor Book, if not introduced by it. I read through the home remedies. Arsenic, morphine, carbolic acid, strong lye, gunpowder and kerosene – all figure prominently in reliable cures, internal and external. Here's the recipe for Mama's sulphur ointment which cured prairie itch: two parts lard, one part sulphur – brimstone. Give the devil some of his own medicine?

I turn to the index and look for prairie itch, but it's not there, so I scan the skin diseases. Oh! Oh!

Scabies: This is an eruption produced by a parasite and is very "catching." It covers the body in parts but is seen chiefly between the fingers where it often makes a raw surface… Sulphur ointment is a sure cure.

When I came home scratching with the prairie itch, Mama put the washtub in the kitchen and I had to bathe not just Saturday, but every night for the rest of the week. And nobody used the water after me. I had caught it, she said, from those dirty children at school.

Mama scrubbed me with lye soap. She towelled me roughly. She applied sulphur ointment. In the morning she insisted I scrub away all scent of sulphur, and she warned me not to scratch at school. As soon as I got home in the afternoon, she applied the salve again. She hauled water from the well and boiled towels, sheets, and any of my clothing that would stand boiling. But never at any time did she hint that I had scabies.

Some years later Mama discovered a super-effective treatment for almost every sore. Phenol is a form of carbolic acid so corrosive that its production is now banned in every country in the world, but the bottle from Mama's phenol and camphor solution is still in her medicine cabinet. She said she was first introduced to it by her dentist when he applied it to her gums after extracting her abscessed teeth in 1934. Common sense told her that it was safe.

It was more effective for some ailments than the best antibiotic is today. A cold sore? One application. Zap! It was gone. Mama never again felt guilty about her children's sores. Whatever harm it did us, Mama was still alive at ninety, with six of her seven children to come at her call.

My grandmother had a whole different set of cures but they too were based on the evil nature of illness and the need to suffer. Grandma's cure for the croup – also in the Doctor Book – was six drops of kerosene on a teaspoon of sugar. After the first treatment, I avoided going to Grandma's when I felt ill. I can still taste the kerosene. For a head cold, Grandma snuffed salt up her nose and hawked and spat, because she knew how to get rid of evil.

Mama did not hawk or spit; she preferred camphor rubs and bed rest. She was good; she did not need to suffer. I too preferred camphor and bed rest, although I was not sure that I was good.

Being good was very important. Children, too young to hide unacceptable behaviour and too young even to talk, were branded as having depraved minds. Either that or they had depraved parents. Somebody was guilty. The Doctor Book says:

> Sometimes the foreskin or the hood of the clitoris is so tight as to cause irritation and keep the passions excited and perhaps they are a cause of masturbation. When such is the case these operations should be performed. Parents should carefully look after these conditions as they, instead of a depraved mind, are the causes of many immoral practices.

When my brother was about seven, he had to have a small operation. It was not necessary for him to stay in the hospital, so the doctor made a house call. He and Mama went into my brother's bedroom, and through the open door I saw the doctor examining my brother's private parts. Mama would never consider a child of hers depraved (the neighbour's rapscallions, yes – but not us), but my brother was still relieved to find that he still had the thing after the operation.

In the chapter "Diseases of Women," the first disease noted is menstruation. No matter how good a girl was, this was one disease she could not avoid. When a girl is "unwell," says the Doctor Book, she is advised to take bed rest and to avoid any strenuous exercise or dancing. She must not study. She is exhorted repeatedly throughout the text not to study.

However,

> A lazy indolent disposition proves likewise very hurtful to a girl at this period. One seldom meets with complaints of menstrual trouble among the properly industrious part of the sex; whereas, the indolent and lazy are seldom free from them. These are in a matter eaten up by greensickness and other diseases of this nature.

I look up greensickness and discover that it is a form of anemia characterized by green pallor, difficult breathing, palpitations and fainting. I doubt that I had anemia, but by the time I reached puberty, I had for so long struggled with the concept of being bad that a sense of unclean guilt smothered me. The shame of menstruation, this mysterious and horrifying body function, tended to make me "unwell." I would have died gladly. I not only felt physically ill, I could not pass the all-important test: I could not look people in the eye.

> Some girls and women seem to be able to do almost anything at this time but such is not the case with many and even those who do not suffer at the time are likely to reap the effects in later life.

Not only were we burdened by "the curse," but also our social life was curtailed by caution. In "A Chapter for Young Women," we are advised:

> Never have anything to do with a young man who is "sowing his wild oats," or who has sown them. This may mean more than you think.

The first time I read that, I wanted to know what I should think. I read the whole book, but I didn't find out. Mama didn't tell me, but she probably knew almost as little.

Many women, when Mama was young, were irresistibly attracted to young men who were "sowing their wild oats." Upon acquiring some slight knowledge in marriage, women could easily become convinced that their husbands had exposed themselves to unmentionable diseases. A good wife did not admit, even to her doctor, that she suspected her husband. The Doctor Book could tell her that her doctor might find it necessary to remove her internal organs – make her no longer a woman – but he would never tell her about the disease, acquired from her husband, that made the operation necessary.

Since many diseases could not be diagnosed, and everything from a headache or rheumatism to paranoia or insanity was attributed to some unmentionable disease, some women spent much of their lives watching for signs of internal rot.

Internal rot was not as great a danger in rural communities as one might think. Roving husbands had a tendency to seek out neighbours whose reserve had broken. People travelled little, so disease had less chance to spread, and if someone was ill, the neighbours knew it. Nonetheless, the birth of a handicapped child was sure to raise questions among neighbours about the sins of the father. Still, it was usually a woman who was condemned.

Women weren't supposed to discuss sex with their daughters any more than with their friends, husbands, or doctors, yet women were responsible for everyone's moral behaviour. When I went out on a date, although money was extremely scarce, Mama provided me with fare home in case I needed it. I found out from my date why I might need it.

Mama never seemed to doubt that I would refrain from any behaviour that was not nice. Grandma, on the other hand, thought it necessary to give me some warning. The first time a young man started hanging around, Grandma was ready. "I see you've got yourself a boyfriend."

"He's not my boyfriend!"

"Well remember, he won't buy a cow if he gets his milk for nothin'."

It was common advice.

Marriage was the romantic goal of every young girl and a necessary achievement in the eyes of her mother. Then again, the unfit had to be weeded out. A "Chapter for Married Women" in the Doctor Book states:

> A woman with poor physical or mental health should not marry, for such a woman as a rule will not bear healthy children. No woman with consumption should marry. Neither should she marry if she has any specific disease… The time will come when the state for its own interest will be compelled to make laws governing marriage. Any mental disease on either or both sides should be sufficient cause for prohibiting marriage, for the offspring of such a marriage

are likely to be endowed with a fearful heritage. Women who intend never to bear or rear children have no right to marry for this means the taking of measures to prevent conception or the getting rid of the product of conception and the latter is, in plain English, abortion.

These words were taken to heart in our small town. Mary, a retarded girl, watched as each of her several sisters acquired a boyfriend, courted, married and had children. Mary had a crush on each boyfriend in turn, and each time, she was told that she musn't have a boyfriend. "I can't get married," she said to me. "I wouldn't be able to look after my children." Mary loved her nieces and nephews dearly.

When the family doctor suggested that Mary could be sterilized, her mother was scandalized. She spent the rest of her life protecting Mary from sin. After she died Mary was taken in by relatives. She moved often, because each home in turn tired of Mary and her search for romance.

Abortion and the Prevention of Conception, which the Doctor Book mentions in that order, are lumped together in two very brief paragraphs.

Abortion is frequently caused by women themselves either by the aid of medicines or mechanical means and, to the shame of my profession, it must be said that there are medical men who do it for the sake of financial gain. Whenever abortion is performed, not only the health but the life of the woman is at stake.

As to the prevention of conception, most of the means used are very injurious and especially so to the woman.

But the book offers no hint on these injurious means. Condoms or douches were sometimes used, but to use them was considered immoral; even to talk about avoiding pregnancy was immoral. Many women, after several births, searched frantically for information on the medicines or mechanical means alluded to in the book, guilt and danger be damned, but to no avail. A woman had to accept the fruits of the original sin. If she did not, she suffered accord-

ingly. Contraception was considered injurious to a woman's health. There is little evidence from those days that women were warned of the effect of repeated pregnancies.

At the age of thirty-two, after the birth of her sixth child, Mama was told by her doctor that it was unwise for her to have any more. I do not remember how I acquired this bit of information, and I cannot imagine how Mama could have learned how to prevent pregnancy. Dispensing birth control information was a criminal offence, and in any event, contraception was something nice women did not talk about. Mama had one more child and both mother and baby did survive.

When I was in my early twenties, I nursed my neighbour, Tina, after what she said was a miscarriage. Tina had been laughing and robust in the spring, but gradually she became more withdrawn. Now in the early fall, she lay in her upstairs bedroom, silent and grey. My ignorance was profound, so my nursing amounted to bringing her hot soup and tea and tending the children. Although her three youngsters needed constant attention, and the clatter from below could not have been reassuring, she heeded her doctor's orders and made no attempt to rise. In the afternoon when I primly brought her tea, she confided that her doctor had told her she was lucky to be alive. "I shouldn't have done it," she wept.

I had no idea what she meant. Shouldn't have done what? Copulate? Use some medicines or mechanical means? I was appalled. I did not ask. "Drink your tea," I said, "and have a nice sleep. You'll feel better when you wake." I thought I should put my arm around her. I couldn't. I poured the tea and fled.

The whole book is not devoted to the frailties of women, however. There is "A Chapter For Men," and it is a masterpiece.

It does not pay for a young man to "sow his wild oats"… Do not expose yourself to these loathsome diseases. However, if you have been exposed, at least observe the laws of cleanliness and immediately wash the exposed parts thoroughly with some good antiseptic solution like carbolic acid, corrosive sublimate or permanganate of potash. Do not wait an hour, or even ten minutes.

Carbolic acid and corrosive sublimate are extremely corrosive, yet there is no word of caution. Permanganate of potash may have been the treatment of choice. At least it wouldn't take the hide off. It would, however, leave the exposed part a bright purple – which would, until the colour faded, jog the conscience and be difficult to explain to the wife. But chances were she never looked at his naked body. Modesty was considered becoming to a woman – especially a wife.

Young men are advised that abstinence and cleanliness are the preventives of these diseases. There is no such advice for women. "Boys will be boys," but a sinning woman was so far beyond the pale she wasn't even mentioned in the Doctor Book. Many women were ignorant about disease, but their fear of becoming pregnant protected them somewhat by pressuring them to resist male attentions.

In Mama's day, and when I was young, women were very aware of the stigma attached to an unwed mother. Even an innocent woman deluded by her swain became a social outcast and fair game for every roving male. I learned about that stigma when Amie, a teenage girl in my home town, became a mother. Amie was hired by Johnny McNeil, a widowed farmer to cook for the threshing crew. The pay was meagre, but the farmer was an attractive man and Amie enjoyed a romantic interlude on her first escape from parental supervision. That is, she enjoyed it until she became pregnant, at which time Johnny's ardor cooled. He denied paternity.

Amie was one of a large family of girls, and the disgrace embraced them all. One day in school, I looked up from my book to see my classmate, Amie's sister, blushing from her hair to her fingertips as the teacher, a middle-aged man, walked away. I didn't know what had happened, but Joan's

discomfort was etched in my memory. She and all of Amie's sisters were helpless – guilty by association. Meanwhile, Johnny basked as the butt of male humour. "I hear the baby has flashing brown eyes," Dad joked. "And beautifully curly hair," Dad's friend countered with a laugh.

An old family friend, even Mama considered Johnny innocent and Amie guilty. A few years later when Johnny married Amie, Mama was unable to forgive him for choosing a fallen woman.

Although the Doctor Book reflected the mores of the time, and was widely used, people did not always follow it slavishly. They trusted to Providence or used common sense, and most communities had women with practical health care knowledge who were willing to help. I may have avoided Grandma's remedies, but many of our neighbours bought her their worries. A mustard plaster cured bronchitis before pneumonia could develop. Soda baths, mud packs or crushed berries relieved many an itch. When the sting of iodine didn't prevent infection, a poultice of bread, soft soap and hot milk drew out the poison.

I remember one time when a woman, the mother of six, had pneumonia and stronger medicine was needed. Grandma caught a fat hen, wrung its neck and bound the warm bird to the woman's chest. There it attracted the woman's disease, which it then carried to the nether world. Grandma returned home at dawn and worked till nightfall, buoyed by the knowledge that the woman's children would not be orphaned.

I sit and think – how did my mother survive? All the guilt instilled by church, folklore and literature, and it was only reinforced by her Doctor Book. One day a few years ago, I had this book in my hand when Mama walked into the room.

"What are you reading now?" she asked.

"Oh Mama!" I sniffed and dabbed my eyes. "I was just looking at the Doctor Book."

"That silly thing," Mama said, "I should have burned it years ago. If you are sick, I'll call Dr. MacLeod." ❖